The Lantern Tower
of Westminster Abbey
1060–2010

Reconstructing its History and Architecture

by

Warwick Rodwell

with a contribution by
Richard Gem

Foreword by
The Dean of Westminster

Oxbow Books
Oxford and Oakville
and
The Dean and Chapter of Westminster

Published by
Oxbow Books, Oxford, UK
for the Dean and Chapter of Westminster

© Oxbow Books, Warwick Rodwell
and the Dean and Chapter of Westminster, 2010

ISBN 978-1-84217-979-6

Westminster Abbey Occasional Papers (series 3), no. 1

A CIP record for this book is available from the British Library

This book is available direct from:

Oxbow Books, Oxford, UK
(Phone: 01865-241249; Fax: 01865-794449)

and

The David Brown Book Company
PO Box 511, Oakville, CT 06779, USA
(Phone: 860-945-9329; Fax: 860-945-9468)

or from our website

www.oxbowbooks.com

Front cover:
*Detail from an oil painting by Pietro Fabris, c. 1735, showing one
of Nicholas Hawksmoor's proposals for building a crossing tower (scheme 4, version iii). WA Lib. Coll.*

Back cover:
Sir Christopher Wren's model of his proposed 400-foot crossing tower and spire, 1710. WA Lib. Coll.

Printed in Great Britain by
Cambrian Printers
Aberystwyth, Wales

Contents

Foreword

by The Very Reverend Dr John Hall, Dean of Westminster

Most of us take our surroundings for granted. We often depend on someone opening our eyes, for example, to the glory of a building about to be lost. John Betjeman's vigorous and successful campaign to save the wonderful St Pancras Station is remembered as creating a turning point in the 1960s in public opinion of Victorian architecture. It was an uphill struggle – but people came to see.

When we do come to see, it is remarkable what we eventually discover. Before I became Dean, I was familiar with the Abbey, but in fact knew little of its architecture or history. I needed a friend's eyes to see the iconic western towers as creatures of the eighteenth century. The stylistic dependence of Barry's Palace of Westminster on the Abbey's Lady Chapel was for me another startling moment of revelation. I remember wondering many years ago why the great crossing of the Abbey church was surmounted by such a stumpy little tower. I came to no conclusion and the thought passed to the back of my mind, to be recalled later when it was again drawn to my attention.

Now we know that the stumpy little tower at the crossing of the Abbey was never intended by anyone. It is simply that the building has never been finished. Now our eyes are open, the Dean and Chapter hope we shall be able to finish the work. We look forward to seeing what might be proposed. This book will greatly help those hoping to make a proposal for the design of a lantern or corona as well as those of us considering what is proposed.

There could be no better guide than Professor Warwick Rodwell, the Abbey's consultant archaeologist, in helping us open our eyes to what has been built at the crossing and what has been proposed at different times in the Abbey's history. In record time, he has detected a great deal of information and drawn persuasive conclusions. His work is a joy to read and will open the eyes of many. We are truly grateful.

Acknowledgements

I am grateful to the Dean of Westminster, the Very Rev'd Dr John Hall, for inviting me to write this account of the history and archaeology of the lantern tower. It could not have been achieved without the generous collaboration of my colleagues at the Abbey: the support and encouragement provided by Sir Stephen Lamport, KCVO (Receiver General) has been invaluable; Dr Tony Trowles (Librarian and Head of the Collections) and Dr Richard Mortimer (Keeper of the Muniments) facilitated access to archives and artefacts for study; Miss Christine Reynolds (Assistant Keeper of the Muniments) was unstinting in her help with searching out and copying documents and illustrations; Clive Richardson (Structural Engineer) kindly shared the results of his investigations and discussed structural issues at length with me; similarly, John Burton (Surveyor of the Fabric) discussed architectural matters with me; and Jim Vincent (Clerk of the Works) provided practical assistance with access and investigation.

Tony Davies and Bill Mowatt of The Downland Partnership expeditiously carried out measured surveys of the crossing with their customary attention to detail, despite the awkward conditions, and Mrs Erica Utsi conducted ground-penetrating radar surveys (GPR) of the floors in the crossing and transepts. Rosie Daswani skilfully undertook the digital cleaning and enhancement of some of the images. Dr Richard Gem, OBE, kindly contributed the appendix to this study and made other helpful suggestions in the text. The manuscript additionally benefitted from the scrutiny of Drs Trowles and Mortimer and Miss Reynolds. For access and permission to study the painting of Westminster Abbey at Woodperry House, I am indebted to Rory Fleming. For further ideas and discussion I must acknowledge Tim Tatton-Brown, Diane Gibbs-Rodwell and Alan Rome, OBE. Finally, my thanks go to David Brown and his colleagues at Oxbow Books for producing this volume so expeditiously: in particular Julie Blackmore, Julie Gardiner and Val Lamb.

The majority of the illustrations are the property and copyright of the Dean and Chapter of Westminster, including those generated by the author; items obtained from other sources are individually credited.

1

Westminster Abbey: the Crossing

The history and architecture of Westminster Abbey have been studied by many scholars, and one might be forgiven for supposing that we know everything there is to know about this great building. But that is far from being the case, and several key features of the Abbey's architecture have disappeared, or have never been completed according to the intentions of their designer. The lantern tower, punctuating the point at which the four arms of the church meet (the crossing), is a case in point. It has a long and extraordinarily complex history. What we see emerging from the roof today is merely the stump of a great architectural feature that has never been completed. [1] Neither its date of construction, nor the reason for its abandonment, has been satisfactorily demonstrated. However, there can be little doubt that it was intended to be a worthy successor to the two previous lantern towers that are known to have existed.

No attempt has hitherto been made to write the history of the crossing tower, but in order to understand the historical and architectural

1 The modern roofscape of Westminster Abbey: aerial view from the south-west. © English Heritage Photo Library

significance of the existing lantern – and to assess what might possibly be done in the future to enhance or complete it – it is first necessary to elucidate how the structure arrived at its present form. That is the result of multiple interventions over a period of 950 years.

2

Edward the Confessor's Crossing Tower and Lantern

The story of the Westminster lantern tower begins much earlier than the present structure, almost one thousand years ago, with Edward the Confessor. Shortly after he ascended the English throne in 1042, he began to rebuild Westminster Abbey in the Romanesque style that was then current in Normandy. At the time of his death in 1066, he had completed the eastern arm, the north and south transepts and half of the nave. A snapshot of Edward's

2 Edward the Confessor's abbey church of the 1060s, from the north, as depicted on the Bayeux Tapestry. The crossing was dominated by a great lantern tower. © Ville de Bayeux

3 Birds-eye view reconstruction of Edward's abbey from the south-west, by Terry Ball, after Richard Gem. WA Lib. Coll.

erected by *c.* 1060, and stood as high above the ridge-line as the roof did above the ground. The tower was probably square in plan, carried on tall, round-headed arches, and was of two main storeys surmounted by a cupola.[1] At the four corners were stair-turrets with conical or pyramidal roofs.[2] [3]

Great towers housing bells, upper-level chapels and other functions were an integral component of nearly all substantial churches in the eleventh century, although their origins were much earlier (see appendix). These towers could be of multiple stages and their materials comprised stone, timber and various metals: the long-established predilection for such structures is well demonstrated, for example, by the Carolingian monastery of Saint-Riquier in Normandy.[3] [111] The Confessor's tower at Westminster was clearly a stone structure, although the cupola and roofs of the turrets would have been of oak, clad with lead sheets. The leadwork itself was probably ornamented, and there may have been additional embellishments using other metals, such as copper and gold. Although the embroiderers' detail on the Bayeux Tapestry must not be interpreted too literally, it is by no means unlikely that the prominent striped effect shown on the cupola represents the decorative treatment of the vertical rolls at the junctions of the lead sheets.

While other cruciform churches in late Anglo-Saxon England certainly possessed towers, these were mostly relatively low structures, as at St Mary-in-Castro, Dover. Edward's tower at Westminster almost certainly represented a level of architectural innovation that was hitherto unseen in the country, and may have borne a resemblance to its closely associated contemporary at Jumièges Abbey in Normandy.

architectural achievement is preserved in the Bayeux Tapestry. This great embroidery, made by English needleworkers in the 1070s (before 1077), depicts the Abbey church from the north, with much of the north wall and transept cut away to reveal the interior. [2] The dominant feature of the building was the crossing tower, which must have been

3

Henry III's Unfinished Crossing Tower

King Henry III devoted a substantial part of his long reign (1216–72) to the reconstruction of Westminster Abbey in the prevailing Gothic style, which was heavily influenced by contemporary building in France. The Confessor's church represented Anglo-Norman architecture and liturgical requirements which, after two hundred years, no longer suited Benedictine needs and aspirations. It was impossible to accommodate the contemporary monastic liturgy in the very short, apsidal eastern arm, let alone find space there to create a shrine in honour of St Edward the Confessor. Reconstruction began in 1220 by adding a large Lady Chapel to the eastern arm, thus creating much more liturgical space. The chapel no longer exists, having been superseded in the early sixteenth century by Henry VII's Lady Chapel [4], but its plan is reconstructible from archaeological evidence.[4]

The extent to which Henry was the initiator of the Abbey's reconstruction is uncertain since the work was begun by the monks, but on such a lavish scale that they quickly ran out of funds. In 1240, Henry stepped in to rescue the situation, and in so doing embarked on what was without doubt the most ambitious and expensive church-building project in English history. The Lady Chapel was completed in 1245, after which the demolition and reconstruction of the eastern arm, crossing and transepts of the old building followed. The work progressed at a staggering rate, so that by the mid-1250s the masonry shell of the eastern parts of the church was complete. The master mason

4 *Westminster Abbey from the east in 1936, showing the emphasis placed on octagonal features in Henry III's original scheme, and further elaborated by Henry VII, whose Lady Chapel appears in the foreground. Almost certainly the square base of the crossing tower was intended to support an impressive octagonal lantern. Henderson 1937*

(architect) was Henry of Reyns, who was well versed in the vocabulary of the latest French Gothic architecture, but was possibly English by nationality.[5] Thus he was presumably the designer of the new crossing tower that replaced King Edward's.

What form of Crossing Tower was envisaged?

It was the norm for major transeptal churches in the early thirteenth century to be provided

with a crossing tower (see appendix). Most often in England that took the form of a low, stone-built lantern that did not project very far above the ridge-lines of the four abutting roofs. These lanterns, which were square in plan, had simple lancet windows in the sides, and were often provided with intra-mural passages and newel-stairs housed in turrets at the corners. Moreover, lanterns were open from the church floor upward, although stone vaults or ceilings were often subsequently inserted at the level of the crossing arches, thus eclipsing the lantern effect (as occurred at Wells, Lichfield and Salisbury cathedrals).

It is generally assumed that early Gothic lantern towers were topped by a pyramidal lead roof, or a timber and lead spire. In most cases, however, the towers have either been totally rebuilt, or raised in height – often in the fourteenth century – to form full-blown crossing towers, capped with stone or timber spires (*e.g.* Salisbury and Lichfield cathedrals), thus removing all evidence for the original termination. Almost certainly the roof structure at Westminster would not have been exposed to view from below, being hidden by either a flat ceiling or a timber vault.

The present diminutive lantern, which

hardly peeps above the ridge-line at Westminster Abbey, clearly owes nothing apart from its square plan to Henry III or Henry of Reyns. So what were their intentions for the design of the crossing at Westminster? Moreover, how much of their tower was actually constructed, and what happened to it? Unfortunately, there is little solid evidence surviving to demonstrate the form of the structure, and none above the point where it emerged through the roof. However, various strands of architectural, archaeological and historical evidence, bolstered by *comparanda* from elsewhere, enable us to make both reasoned deductions and educated guesses. We must not, however, be seduced by some older artistic reconstructions which, though exquisite in themselves, are more representative of mid-fourteenth-century Salisbury than of Westminster a century earlier.[6] [5]

First, we should consider the overall design of the thirteenth-century abbey church as an indicator of the type of lantern tower that it is likely to have borne. Not only were important elements of the monastic liturgy performed in the crossing but, uniquely in England, this was – and still is – also the location where the coronation of monarchs takes place. It is therefore inconceivable that Henry would have considered a squat lantern with a simple pyramidal roof as an appropriate treatment for the crossing, especially since he was attempting to outshine the contemporary Gothic architecture of France. Moreover, he was demolishing the lofty and clearly impressive tower raised by King Edward, and the successor to this needed to be no less worthy. The new nave was destined to be the tallest in England, and it needed to be surmounted by a lantern tower that made a clear architectural statement. This deduction is confirmed, *a fortiori*, when the Abbey is viewed from the east. [4] If we ignore the elaborate decoration of Henry VII's Chapel – but not the physical presence of a large apsidal chapel here, since there was one from 1220 onward – the multi-tiered composition of the church's architectural form is immediately apparent. More than that, all the higher elements point upwards to heaven in a most demonstrative fashion: the sanctuary roof, the high gables of the transepts and the pinnacled corner-turrets. They all demand a pointed centrepiece standing high above the crossing. The inadequacy of anything akin to the present stumpy lantern to provide that focus requires no emphasizing. Henry's lantern tower needed to be both tall and capped by either a spire or a high-pointed roof.

Although up to parapet level the crossing was square in plan, it does not follow that the tower had to continue above the roof in the same form. Indeed, a large square tower would not have been congruent with the rest of the building, and outwardly would now give the appearance of being a later medieval addition. It can be ruled out as an option. One of the most striking features of Henry's design was the ubiquitous use of octagons and half-octagons. The chapter house, described by the contemporary chronicler Matthew Paris as 'beyond compare', was octagonal. The terminations of the new Lady Chapel, and the presbytery and its ambulatory were all half-octagons, while the four two-storey chapels attached to the ambulatory had the form of octagonal apses. Even stair-turrets and pinnacles were eight-sided. It is therefore plausible to conclude that the lantern tower above roof level should have been octagonal too. The eastern view of Westminster must have borne a striking resemblance to that of Amiens Cathedral, although the latter was endowed with a greater *chevet* of apsidal chapels.[8] [6] It is not certain what crowned the crossing at Amiens in the thirteenth century, the present two-staged lantern and needle-like *flèche* dating from 1528. But again the architecture demands an octagonal lantern or spire.

Existing Evidence

The Westminster crossing is square in plan, measuring 44¼ ft (13.5 m).[9] [7, 8A] The piers comprise an octagonal core of Purbeck marble with four massive, attached shafts on the cardinal faces, and four smaller ones on the diagonal faces. Interspersed between these are eight further small shafts also attached to the core of the pier. [9] All the shafts have moulded bases, and the complete ensemble stands on a high octagonal plinth. The piers are freestanding for one-third of their height, *i.e.* up to arcade-capital level, whereupon they engage with the ashlar masonry of the triforium and above that the clearstorey. [8B, 12] A single shaft-ring marks the point of transition. [11] The shafts have well moulded capitals, also in Purbeck marble. Rising from these are the four huge, pointed crossing arches

which are heavily moulded and probably of Caen stone.[10] [10] This fine-grained limestone from Normandy was extensively employed for moulded and carved work in Henry's abbey.

The slenderness of the crossing piers, relative to their great height, has suggested to some commentators that a massive tower rising several storeys above the roof, and crowned by a stone spire, was neither envisaged nor capable of being supported, although Sir Christopher Wren clearly thought otherwise: p. 29, and modern engineering calculations have confirmed that such a structure was sustainable (p. 90). Nevertheless, the emphasis was probably on providing a lantern tower, rather than a bell tower. In the thirteenth century many of the greater churches were augmented with a fashionable *campanile*, an entirely separate structure which housed the major bells. Westminster Abbey possessed one

6 Amiens Cathedral from the south-east, showing an array of octagonal-apsidal components and the lantern and flèche of 1528. J. Feuillie/ CNMHS/SPADEM

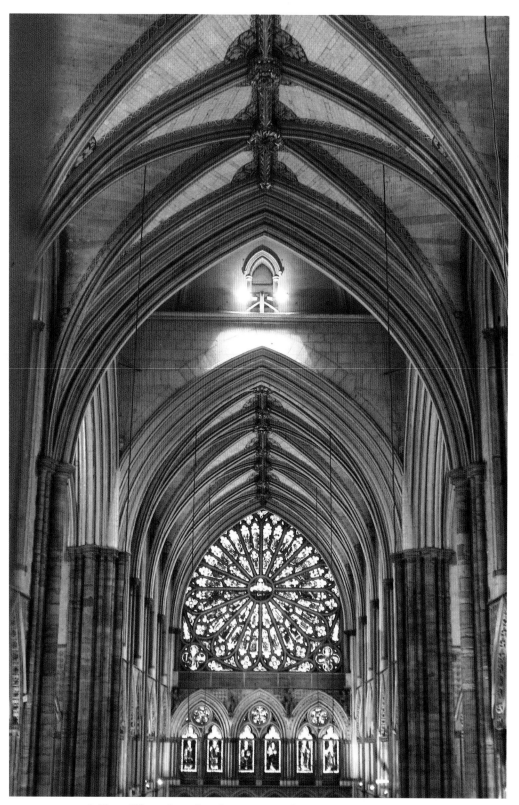

7 Henry III's crossing and north transept, viewed from the south transept. Author

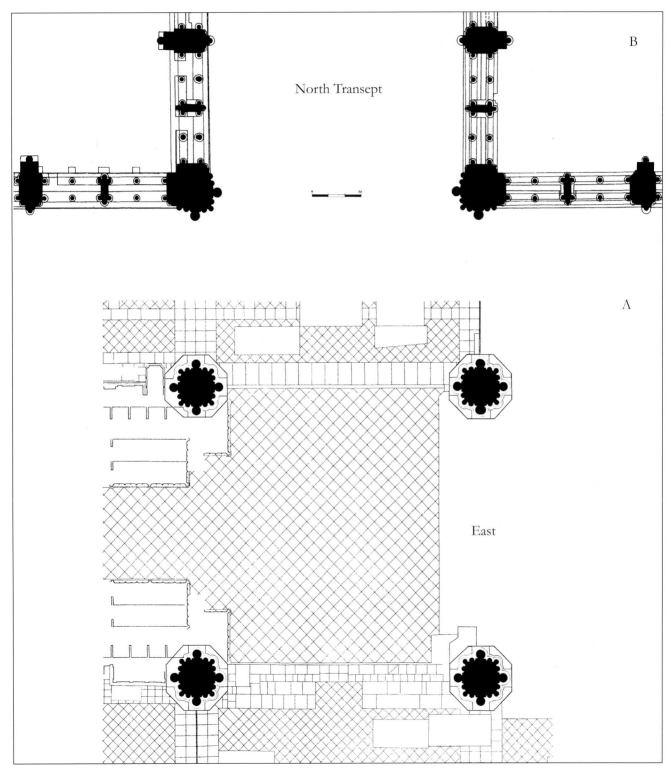

North Transept

B

A

East

8 A (lower). Plan of the crossing at quire pavement level. B (upper). Plan of the northern side of the crossing and the first bay of the north transept at triforium level. North is at the top. Scale of 3 m. The Downland Partnership

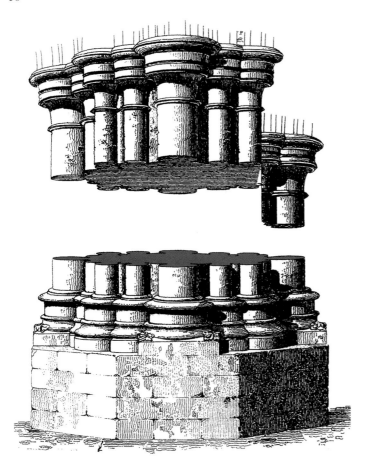

and it stood to the north-west of the church, on the site later occupied by the Middlesex Guildhall (now Supreme Court of the United Kingdom).[11] It was an elaborate structure, square at the base and with a staged octagonal superstructure. The *campanile*, which was demolished in 1750, is shown in Wyngaerde's view of Westminster. [30] There was a closely similar bell tower in a comparable location at Salisbury Cathedral, and that was demolished in 1790. Again on the north-west, Chichester Cathedral has a somewhat later *campanile*, which still stands.

All that remains today in the crossing of the mid-thirteenth-century work are the four great arches and some of the masonry comprising the internal angles of the tower at the lowest level. [10, 11, 12] Nothing dating from this period is visible externally. However, there are four original stone corbels in the form of human heads, set low down in the corners of the lantern, just above the point where the crossing arches meet one another.[12] Each head supports a Purbeck marble base which was designed to carry a small, free-standing corner-shaft. [13] This confirms that the ubiquitous marble shafting in the Abbey was intended to

9 *Details of the Purbeck marble capital and base of the south-west crossing pier, drawn in 1822. Neale and Brayley 1823*

10 *The upper part of the crossing and junction of the arches. View west. Author*

11 (far left) East elevation of the interior of the crossing and lantern tower. The Downland Partnership

12 (left) The top of the south-east crossing pier and springing of the arches. Author

13 Detail of the north-east crossing pier with a corbel in the form of a male head supporting a Purbeck marble base; the latter was intended to carry a detached shaft, rising in the angle of the lantern. Author

continue inside the lantern tower, but that is as far as the physical evidence takes us. Doubtless there were capitals on the tops of the shafts, although how high they rose is indeterminable. Also, what did the capitals support? Most likely, they carried small vaults which decorated the underside of the corbelling or the squinches that would have been necessary at the corners of the crossing, if the lantern above was octagonal in plan (p. 13).

How much of the Lantern Tower was actually built?

The critical question is: was Henry's tower ever built above roof level? Since nothing attributable to the thirteenth century appears to survive today at eaves level or above, there has long been a presumption of the negative. However, the crossing had to be finished, whether temporarily or permanently, in a way that provided a satisfactory, watertight junction between it and the four abutting roofs of the presbytery, nave and transepts.[13] The framing

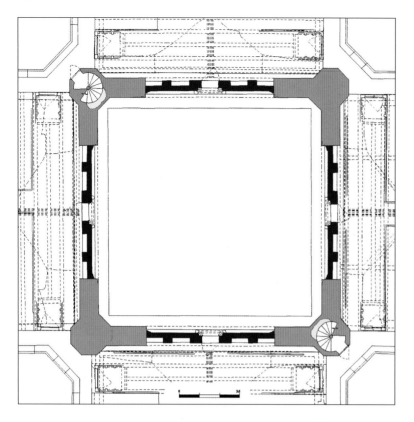

14 Plan of the lantern tower at main eaves level, with the adjoining parapet walks and high roofs. Key: yellow, medieval; orange, Hawksmoor, 1724–27; maroon, Wyatt, 1803–05. North is at the top. Scale of 3 m. The Downland Partnership and author

of the four high roofs also relied on a solid central feature to retain the trussed-rafters in an upright position. If the intention had been to erect a square tower, then the masonry of the crossing would almost certainly have been taken up to ridge level, thus providing the essential abutments for the roofs. The resultant structure, if left unfinished at that point, would have had an appearance closely similar to what we see today. The fact that the present squat lantern does not have thirteenth-century walls provides a strong argument that it was not originally square in plan above eaves level. However, the possibility of an alternative scenario must be considered, namely that the square tower rose to ridge level, converting to an octagon thereafter, but a later modification involved lowering the corners and beginning the octagon at eaves level. Moreover, there is a further complication to take into account: two of the eighteenth-century corner-turrets embody vertical columns of medieval ashlar masonry that clearly belonged to earlier stair-turrets. [**14**] Whether that work dates from Henry III's period, or slightly later, is uncertain, but it confirms unequivocally that a medieval tower once stood at least to the height of the present one.[14]

We know for certain that Henry III did not live to see his lantern tower finished, because a temporary ceiling had to be erected over the crossing two years after his death for the joint coronation of his son, Edward I, and Queen Eleanor, on 19th August 1274. What was described as the 'new tower over the quire' had to be 'boarded up'.[15] Henry's failure to finish the lantern is easily explained in terms of building logistics. Having completed the crossing and transepts in the late 1250s, the priority in the 1260s would have been to press on with the reconstruction of the nave, and only when that had been completed would the masons have returned to build the crossing tower or lantern. Work on that could proceed at a later date from scaffolding erected externally, and the provision of a temporary ceiling over the crossing would ensure that building operations did not interfere with monastic observance below. Meanwhile, the emerging first stage of the lantern tower would simply have been provided with a temporary, low-pitched roof. A decorative ceiling may well have been inserted inside, even though it was a relatively short-term measure. The painted timber ceiling at Peterborough Cathedral, dating from the early part of Henry III's reign, or that of his Painted Chamber in the Palace of Westminster (destroyed by fire, 1834), hint at what might have covered the crossing in the Abbey.

Hence, all the evidence points to the lantern having never been finished in the thirteenth century: the walls were taken up only to a sufficient height to form abutments for the four high roofs. We must return again to the question of the plan of the lantern tower, since that is not wholly resolved. The crossing piers and arches define a square up to eaves level, but what rose above that, to ridge level and beyond?[16] If the first stage of the tower, from eaves to ridge level, was square, then how do we explain the absence today of thirteenth-century masonry at the four angles? Externally, all visible masonry is eighteenth century, as it also is internally, except for the first 2.0 m of Reigate ashlar above each of the corbels in the corners (already mentioned). The present interface is at such a low level (far below the eaves) [**15**] that it cannot represent the point at which Henry's masons stopped building: it would have been impossible to weatherproof the structure at this level. Hence, it can only mean that some thirteenth-century masonry has been taken

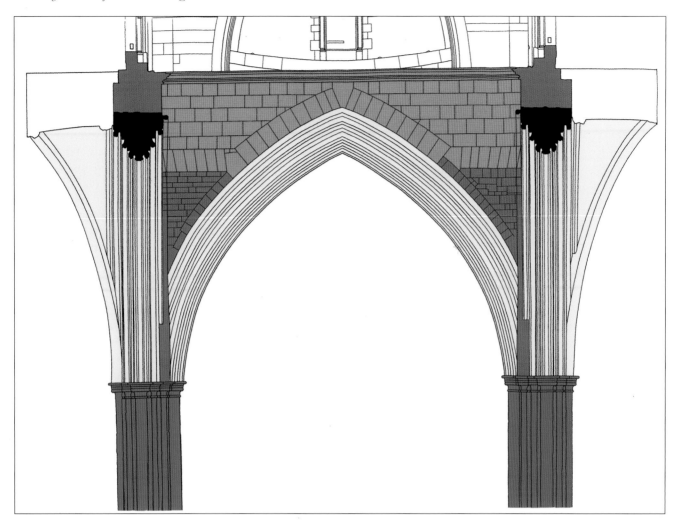

down, to well below roof level, and then the walls have been built up again. The interface between the two periods of work is so clear and consistent in all four corners that something much more fundamental than the repair of a localized failure is implied. [59] So what could have been the motivation for demolishing all four original corners of the tower?

It has already been argued on stylistic grounds that the lantern stage is more likely to have been octagonal in plan than square. If this is accepted, then there is an inevitable corollary: the four salient angles of the crossing had to be merged into the diagonal faces of the lantern stage just above the level of the high vaults. In the Middle Ages, the transition from four to eight sides was normally effected either by corbelling or by constructing diagonal arches (squinches) across the corners of the tower; and upon those supports the four angled sides of the octagon were then raised.

The level at which the surviving thirteenth-century masonry ceases coincides exactly with the position from which the squinches, or corbelling, would be expected to spring. The evidence that there was once an octagonal lantern tower, supported on the side-walls and the corbelled angles of the crossing, is thus compelling. The removal of those angled supports in the sixteenth century, and the subsequent making-good of the masonry at the corners of the crossing, gave us what we have today (below, p. 51). The transition from a square crossing to an octagonal lantern is well demonstrated by the corbelled arrangement at Coutances Cathedral in Normandy.[17] [16, 17]

Hence, circumstantial, architectonic and archaeological evidence all combine to suggest that Henry's masons constructed an octagonal base for the intended lantern stage on top of the walls of the crossing. Once that had been achieved, there would have been solid

15 East crossing arch, showing the survival of mid-thirteenth-century masonry. Key: green, Purbeck marble piers; khaki, spandrels; yellow, arch and vault mouldings. Hawksmoor's masonry of 1725–27 is shown in orange. The disposition is similar in the other three crossing arches. The Downland Partnership and author

16 Coutances Cathedral. View east through the crossing, showing the base of the octagonal lantern and the corbelling that carries its diagonal faces. Bony 1951

17 (below) Coutances Cathedral. The crossing tower viewed from below, showing the corbelled supports, galleried basement stage, lantern with sixteen windows and the ribbed vault with a bell-manhole. Bony 1951

abutments for the high roofs, making everything complete and watertight up to ridge level. The open top of the octagon would have been given a temporary roof while building progressed on more urgent fronts elsewhere. When Henry III died in 1272, work on the new abbey was halted, and only the first five bays of the nave had been reconstructed in the Gothic style. The momentum was never regained and the nave was not finished for another two hundred years, and it was nearly five hundred years before the western towers assumed their present form under Nicholas Hawksmoor (p. 63). Small wonder, then, that work on the lantern tower was not resumed for a considerable time.

Fortuitously, there is a potential illustration of the octagonal base of the Henrician lantern in a Tudor drawing of the Abbey. [20, 22] The architectural significance of this source seems to have been largely overlooked by previous scholars, or dismissed as imaginary.[18] The drawing is discussed in detail in the next chapter, but here it is relevant to note that two periods of construction are potentially indicated, one being thirteenth century and the other late medieval. Stylistically, it is obvious from its architectural form that the crenellated upper part of the lantern and the cupola could not date from the mid-thirteenth century, but there is no reason why the octagonal base upon which they were founded should not have been of that era. Thus, we may propose with some confidence that when Henry III died the crossing of his new church was surmounted by an octagonal stone plinth, 13.4 m (44 ft) across, upon which it was intended to erect a lantern tower befitting the grandeur of the rest of the building.

Like so much else at Westminster, the lost design was doubtless heavily influenced by contemporary French architecture. France already had a long tradition of building octagonal crossing towers, some of which were of extreme monumentality, such as Romanesque Toulouse, or early Gothic Coutances. At Westminster, aesthetics would probably have demanded that the tower comprised two lantern stages of stone construction (as in the Romanesque Notre Dame at Clermont-Ferrand). But here we run out of direct evidence and can only resort to speculation. Above the second stage might well have been a construction in timber and lead. The French were also noted for their predilection for crowning roofs and lanterns

with lightweight openwork structures, often culminating in tall, needle-like *flèches*. The cathedral of Notre Dame, Paris, has just such a feature over the crossing: it comprises an octagonal basement, two openwork lantern stages and an immensely tall *flèche*. While the present structure is a mid-nineteenth-century recreation by Viollet-le-Duc, its medieval predecessor is depicted in a drawing of *c.* 1530.[19] [18, 19]

Gaining Access to the Lantern Stage

Before leaving the subject of Henry III's lantern, the issue of access needs to be addressed. There are newel stairs in the outermost corners of the transepts, rising to parapet level. Provision had then to be made for getting from the main parapet walks into the lantern, and thence into its roof or spire. French octagonal lantern towers were normally accompanied by four turrets rising from the corners of the crossing below, and one or more of these would contain a newel stair. The turrets could be either integrated with the diagonal sides of the octagon, or freestanding

18 (far left) Notre Dame Cathedral, Paris. Detail from a birds-eye view of the Ile de la Cité, from the west, drawn c. 1530. It shows the medieval octagonal lantern and a tall flèche rising above the crossing. © Musée Notre-Dame

19 (left) Notre Dame Cathedral, Paris. Viollet-le-Duc's reconstructed two-stage lantern and flèche. Erlande-Brandenberg 1999

(with a short flier or other form of link to effect the stair connection). The Tudor drawing shows no stair-turret at the north-west corner, only the shouldering at the transition of the square to the octagon. Consequently, we can be certain that in the early sixteenth century the Westminster lantern was not flanked by a quartet of stair-turrets. But that does not imply that none were intended in Henry III's church.

The resolution to this conundrum is happily provided through a combination of Sir Christopher Wren's observations, and archaeology. In his report on the Abbey in 1713, Wren stated: 'The original intention was plainly to have had a steeple [*i.e.* a tower], the beginnings of which appear on the corners of the cross[ing], but left off before it rose so high as the ridge of the roof'.[20] Remains of the thirteenth-century corner-turrets were still extant and had commanded Wren's attention: confirmation of this appears in his drawing of 1715, showing the plan and internal elevation of the upper part of the crossing. He showed detached octagonal turrets at the corners, two of which (north-west and south-east) contained newel stairs.[21] [**31**] Wren had intended to rebuild these. In the event, it fell to Hawksmoor to reconstruct them in 1726–27, although not as freestanding turrets: he incorporated them in the corners of a square lantern of his own design (p. 53).

Not only do the angle-turrets have their ancestry in the thirteenth century but, as noted above, careful examination of the ashlar lining inside both the south-east and north-west turrets has revealed medieval masonry *in situ*. [**14**] Part of the curving internal wall of the stair has survived, almost up to the level of the roof ridges, where it was incorporated in the later structure. This confirms that the lower sections of at least two – and presumably all four – of the detached corner-turrets were built. Thus, when Henry III died, the crossing of Westminster Abbey would have been crowned by the basement stage of an octagonal lantern and the stumps of four detached corner-turrets: all would have spawned temporary cappings.

4

The Late Medieval Stone and Timber Lantern

The earliest datable view of Westminster Abbey is a drawing contained in Abbot John Islip's obituary roll of 1532.[22] The roll embodies five drawings in all, the one of interest for the present enquiry being the illuminated letter 'U' for a text which was intended to begin with the word *Universis*. [20] However, the remainder of the membrane is blank, since the text was never inscribed and the initial (like the other four drawings) was never coloured. The artist is believed to have been Gerard Horenbouts of Ghent, who was Court Painter to Henry VIII.[23]

Taken from the north-west, the view retrospectively depicts the coronation of King Henry VIII in 1509, at which Islip officiated. Here, we unmistakably see the crossing topped by a crenellated octagonal lantern tower, quite low, and rising out of its centre is an octagonal cupola. [21, 22] The Islip drawings are minutely detailed and the representation of the lantern displays too much verisimilitude to be dismissed as a mere flourish. In particular, the care taken by the artist to delineate the north-west 'shoulder' of the crossing – which marks the structural transition from square to octagon, and is an external expression of the squinch arch (or internal corbelling) – is a powerful argument that he was actually looking at the church when he drew this view.

The Evidence of the Drawing in the Islip Roll

The Islip Roll drawing confirms that, sometime before 1532, a crenellated lantern stage was constructed on the octagonal base, and that the incipient turrets had been dispensed with, leaving behind only a small amount of masonry that was integral with the diagonal faces of the octagon. The details in the drawing are somewhat sketchy, but still nevertheless

20 Decorated initial letter 'U' from Abbot Islip's funerary roll (1532), depicting the coronation of Henry VIII in 1509. It shows a lantern over the crossing and building works in progress on the western towers. Drawing attributed to Gerard Horenbouts. WAM Lib. Coll.

21 Detail of the octagonal lantern over the crossing, depicted in the Islip Roll, 1532. WAM Lib. Coll.

22 Sketch to illustrate the construction details of the lantern tower, based on the drawing in the Islip Roll. Author

octagonal cupola

crenellated parapet
corbel-table

octagonal lantern

roof ridge

S = shoulder over
squinch-arch

transept and nave parapet

to illuminate the upper region of the crossing, while the cupola may have housed one or more bells.

Although Westminster was superficially much plainer, the illustrated structure bears more than a passing resemblance to the octagon over the crossing at Ely Cathedral, which was erected between 1322 and 1342.[25] [23] But with an overall plan dimension of *c.* 23.8 m (78 ft), it was approaching twice the size of Westminster's octagon. Closer in scale was the former octagonal lantern at Peterborough Cathedral, where the crossing that it crowned is 15.25 m (50 ft) square. There, the low tower, which was rebuilt in the mid-fourteenth century, had octagonal corner-turrets and was surmounted by a crenellated timber lantern stage which doubtless once supported a tall lead-covered timber spire. [24] The spire had gone before 1656, and the octagon was demolished in the late eighteenth century.[26] Thus, Ely and Peterborough – both major Benedictine abbeys – provide precedent for the construction of an octagonal lantern tower at Westminster, from the mid-fourteenth century.

These are by no means the only examples: the Blackfriars' church at Norwich had a two-stage octagonal stone lantern, and there are numerous parallels for staged octagonal lanterns on a much

23 Ely Cathedral from the north-east, showing its fourteenth-century octagonal stone and timber lantern tower. Drawn by John Harris, c. 1720. Willis 1742

24 Peterborough Cathedral from the north-east, showing the square crossing tower and remains of the fourteenth-century octagonal lantern that surmounted it. Drawn by John Harris, c. 1720. Willis 1742

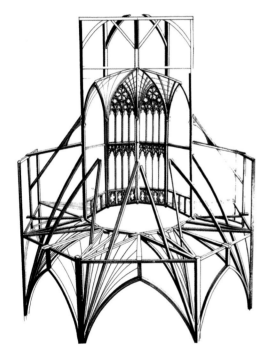

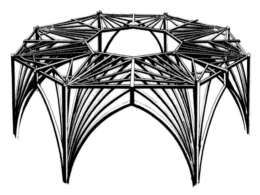

25 (far left) Ely Cathedral. The timber skeleton of the octagon. Hewett 1985

26 (left) Ely Cathedral. The timber roof-deck and vaulting which supports the upper lantern. The same kind of structure would have been required inside the stone octagon at Westminster Abbey. Hewett 1985

smaller scale in the high and later Middle Ages. They occur variously in masonry and timber, and in a combination of materials. Inside the masonry shell at Westminster would have been a timber-framed structure which served three functions: a deck to support the lead roof, a base upon which to seat the cupola, and a timber vault (doubtless decorated in imitation of masonry) forming the ceiling of the lantern. In essence, the basic framing cannot have been very different from that inside the octagon at Ely, although the latter being larger and more ornate, required extra bracing. [25, 26] Also, the cupola at Ely is considerably more complex in design.[27] Elaborate timber constructions broadly of the Ely type were common on the continent: having begun in the Carolingian period, their derivatives were still being erected in the sixteenth century. These lanterns were not an uncommon sight in France down to the

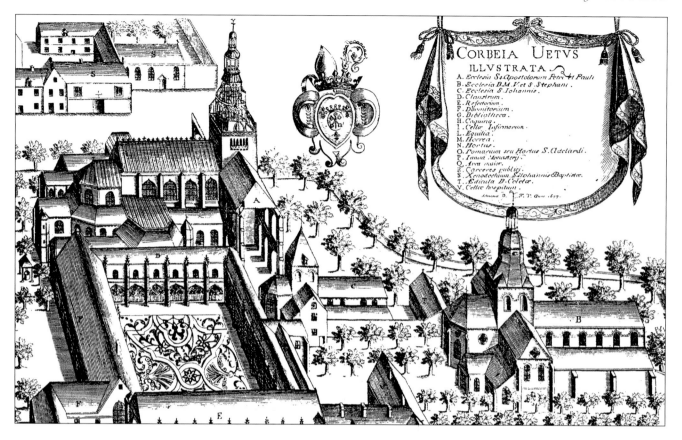

*27 Corbie Abbey,
Normandy. View of
1677, showing an
elaborate medieval timber
and lead openwork crown
on the west tower of the
abbey church, and an
octagonal lead roof and
cupola over the lantern
tower of the subsidiary
church of SS Mary and
Stephen. Peigné-Delacourt
1871*

eighteenth century, as for example at Corbie abbey.[28] [27]

The construction of the crenellated stone lantern at Westminster Abbey could hardly been earlier than the mid-fourteenth century, while the cupola perhaps points more towards a fifteenth-century date. Superficially, the windows suggest the same century, but this may be placing too much reliance on sketchy detail. No documented sources for the construction, or the presence, of a lantern tower have been noted, but since the subject has never been seriously considered hitherto, it is possible that oblique references to such a structure may have been overlooked. Given that the momentum to demolish the western half of the Romanesque nave, and to replace it with a continuation of the early Gothic work of the eastern bays, had been lost with the death of Henry III, by the mid-fourteenth century it might have seemed logical to finish the crossing first, before embarking on further demolition. A special 'New Work' fund had been set up in 1335, ostensibly to repair damage to the monastic offices caused by a fire in 1298. However, in 1341–43 the

fund was being applied to the repair of the eleventh-century part of the nave, suggesting that its replacement with a new structure was not considered imminent. This represents the earliest date at which consideration of finishing the lantern tower might have become a reality (possibly inspired by the recent completion of Ely's octagon).

A decision to revive the rebuilding project on Westminster's nave did not come until 1375, and in 1387 the New Work fund was made available solely for this project. Henry Yeveley, the prolific royal architect, was appointed to superintend the reconstruction, and it is tempting to see Yeveley's hand in the completion of the lantern tower: he died in 1400.

Access to the Lantern Stage

One potential problem remains to be considered: how was access gained to the parapet and lead roof of the lantern, and thence to the cupola? The Islip drawing shows no stair-turret at the north-west corner (the only one visible), and thus it can be deduced that the later medieval lantern was not provided with a suite of corner-

28 Reconstruction of Westminster Abbey in c. 1537, showing an octagonal lantern and cupola over the crossing, as seen in the Islip Roll (1532). Drawing by Henderson, 1936. WA Lib. Coll.

turrets. [21] However, the possibility that there was one low-key turret – provided for purely functional reasons – cannot be discounted. It has already been noted that the incipient Henrician turret housed a stair at the south-east angle (p. 21), confirming that there was the potential for a small stair-turret at one corner of the crossing; this would have facilitated access from the parapet walk on the east side of the transept to the roof and upper part of the octagonal lantern. A single stair-turret attached to one angle of a tower is a typical feature of English medieval churches, and is found on both western towers and crossing towers.

A proposal to replace the late medieval lantern in the early sixteenth century is mentioned by two historians. First, Henry Keepe, writing in 1683, tells us that John Islip (abbot, 1500–32) 'designed a stately tower and lanthorn, with a goodly chime of bells to be placed therein, over the midst of the cross of this church; but finding the foundation of the old pillars too weak to support his structure, the bells were set up in one of the western towers, where they remain to this day'.[29] Another historian, John Dart, writing in 1723, tells a similar story, although the content differs somewhat from Keepe's account: 'There was indeed a design in Abbot Islip's time of a middle tower and spire, but the pillars, curiously taper, and very lofty, were thought too weak for such a weight; so that the work remained unfinished'.[30] Regrettably, the source of Dart's information is now lost, but it may have been oral tradition.

These two accounts would appear to complement one another, rather than duplicate information; additionally, we may suspect that there is yet more to the story than has come down to us. The purchase of bells implies that there must have been an existing tower in which it was proposed to hang them. The initial intention may have been to haul them up to the octagonal lantern, where there may already have been a medieval bell. It is difficult to envisage how a bell-frame containing a ring of six could have been accessibly installed and conveniently rung in the lantern, without inserting floors, and thus destroying the ability of the tower to function as a lantern at all.[31] Perhaps it was intended to install solid floors in the tower, as had happened in many other churches by this time. However, when it was found that this was either impracticable, or not structurally safe, the proposal to construct a new tower and spire that could properly

5

The Disappearance of the Medieval Lantern

The Fate of the Lantern Tower

The lantern does not appear in any view of the Abbey after 1532, and it was presumably lost shortly after that date (or perhaps even earlier: see p. 24). It is improbable that the loss resulted purely from the decay of the carpentry, but a fire caused either accidentally or by a lightning strike could have precipitated destruction. However, it is inherently unlikely that an incident as major as this would have passed without being noticed in the written record, and we should perhaps seek another cause. Structural failure in the crossing was reported by Wren when he carried out a survey in 1713, and this was potentially the problem that precipitated the removal of the lantern (see below, p. 31).

Wren recorded that the crossing piers had all bowed, and the adjacent arches of the triforium arcades were fractured. Later references to the necessary repairs imply that the crossing arches were also distressed, which must inevitably have occurred if the piers themselves had moved to any significant extent. The date at which this failure occurred cannot be precisely established, but it was well before the eighteenth century. If the corbelling or squinch-arches carrying the four angled sides of the masonry octagon had fractured, then the whole superstructure would have been endangered. Structural measurements and archaeological observations indicate that movement of the north-west crossing pier caused the principal damage. The most expeditious method of dealing with the problem was simply to demolish the lantern.

If the crossing piers and arches were failing in the early sixteenth century, it would have been an understandable reaction to remove as much weight as possible from them, in the belief (albeit mistaken) that this was the cause of the problem. In reality, it may have exacerbated the situation. We shall return to this subject later (p. 58).

A view of the Abbey from the east, formerly attributed to Wenceslaus Hollar and assigned to *c.* 1630, has recently been redated to the mid-sixteenth century.[34] Its depiction of the Abbey's roofscape is very revealing. It does not show any upstanding feature over the crossing, but a low-pitched roof linking the ridges of the nave and eastern arm; the south transept roof stands independently, in an ungainly manner, and with a V-shaped gap, or gusset, between it and the main east–west roof. [**29**] Presumably, there was a similar feature on the north side

29 Anonymous, mid-sixteenth century. Detail from a drawing showing Westminster Abbey from the east, with a temporary configuration of roofs over the crossing after the medieval lantern had been removed. This view appears also to show a fragment of the lower part of the south-east stair-turret. © Victoria and Albert Museum: E.128–1924

*30 Van den Wyngaerde,
c. 1544.*

*A (upper). Detail from
his original Panorama,
showing Westminster
Abbey and Hall from the
north-east. No tower or
other feature is indicated
over the crossing.* ©
*Bodleian Library,
Oxford.*

*B (lower). Mid-
nineteenth-century
redrawing of his birds-eye
view of Westminster
Abbey from the north-
east, showing a box-
lantern over the crossing
which does not appear in
the original illustration.
Mitton 1908*

Early Views of the Abbey

The next piece in the Tudor jigsaw comes from the birds-eye view of Westminster by Anthonis van den Wyngaerde, which forms part of his *Panorama of London*, drawn in *c.* 1544.[36] **[30A]** Since the original drawing is very faint, it was copied and engraved several times in the nineteenth century,[37] and one version in particular has frequently been reproduced in subsequent works.[38] It shows the Abbey with a square 'box-lantern', projecting slightly above the ridges of the four main roofs. The lantern has a plain coping and a pyramidal roof of low pitch. There are two small windows in each face, but no stair-turrets at the angles. **[30B]** Superficially, the structure depicted could be mistaken for the present lantern, except for the absence of corner-turrets. However, there are major discrepancies between the two versions of the drawing, since Wyngaerde's original does not show anything projecting from the roof of the Abbey church. In fact, it is extremely sketchy, and the only prominent detail is the pinnacled gable of the north transept; its counterpart on the south is also depicted with a tall finial. Numerous alterations and introductions of non-original material are found in the Victorian re-drawing, and the 'box-lantern' is wholly fictitious, being merely a re-working of Hawksmoor's tower.[39]

To recapitulate: there are fortuitously three views of the Abbey, all dating to the first half of the sixteenth century and showing the crossing in markedly different states. Although the Islip drawing dates from 1532, it records an event which took place in 1509, when there was a staged lantern tower.[40] The second drawing is undated, but appears to record the transition between the destruction of the octagonal lantern and the reroofing of the crossing. The third illustration, dating from *c.* 1544, shows the Abbey church without any feature on its roof.

Various views of Westminster Abbey dating from the seventeenth century exist, and none shows anything projecting from the roof above the crossing. Hollar's north and south prospects (1654), for example, simply depict the four main roof-ridges all meeting over the centre of the crossing.[41] Neither does a lantern appear on Keirincx's prospect of Westminster (1625),[42] nor on Hollar's general views, although a small feature that seems to be a roof dormer occurs in the north-east angle of his drawing of

too. The anonymous artist is most unlikely to have invented this incongruous arrangement of junctions between the roofs: arguably, he captured the moment when all the timber and much of the masonry of the lantern had been taken down, and a low-pitched, temporary roof covering had been, or was being, installed over the crossing. The arrangement depicted in this view could not have obtained for long, and it would certainly not have stood like this since the 1250s. In the first place, it would have been well nigh impossible to keep the crossing (and hence the quire) watertight, but even more significant is the fact that, being entirely without lateral support from a crossing tower, the trussed rafters of the transept roofs were very vulnerable: they would have racked within a few years, and partial collapse would doubtless have ensued. The original design of the transept roofs necessitated their being supported at both ends by masonry (*i.e.* by the crossing tower and the transept gables, respectively).[35]

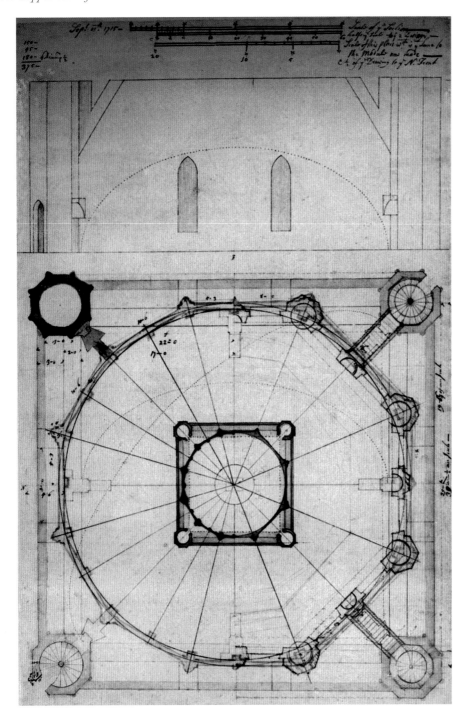

31 Wren, 1715. Plan of the crossing at eaves level, as then existing, showing the bases of the thirteenth-century angle-turrets and a pair of narrow openings in each wall (east is at the top). Overdrawn on this are two alternative versions for a proposed spire (dodecagonal on the left, and octagonal on the right), and in the centre is a plan at a smaller scale, showing the proposed arrangement of the parapets at the top of the tower. Also on the same sheet is an internal elevation of the east side of the crossing, as modified in the sixteenth century; the dotted line represents a ceiling of elliptical form. Bodleian Library, Oxford: Gough Mss. Wren Society 1934

1647.[43] Thus, the evidence seems conclusive: the later medieval lantern and at least some of the masonry of the thirteenth-century octagonal base upon which it sat were removed sometime between *c.* 1509 and 1544, and, after an initial patching-up of the crossing, a new roof was erected to infill the space and connect effectively with the four abutting high roofs.

The Earliest Architects' Drawings

However, the story may not be quite as straightforward as it appears because various features relict from the former lantern are recorded in two architects' drawings of the early eighteenth century, and from these further details of its construction can be gleaned. The first is a plan of the crossing at eaves level, made in 1715, overlaid upon which is Wren's proposal to build a tower and spire.[44] [**31**] The walls of the crossing were each pierced by a pair of narrow, lancet-headed openings (60 cm wide). These never functioned as windows because they were set low in the walls, were unsplayed and opened only into the adjacent roof spaces. They were almost certainly associated with the thirteenth-century construction, and are suggestive of a gallery around the interior of the crossing, at the base of the lantern stage.[45]

The plan is accompanied by an internal elevation of the east side of the upper part of the crossing, from which additional important details can be gleaned. It shows that the walls and octagonal corner-turrets stood to a height of 18 ft (5.5 m) above eaves level, and that the crossing was capped with its own roof. That was noted by Wren as being of chestnut, and it comprised two trusses intersecting at right-angles, anchored by wall-posts rising from corbels at the centre of each side. Although certainty cannot obtain, the structure gives the appearance of being sixteenth or perhaps seventeenth century in date. The crossing was ceiled with a plaster dome of elliptical profile, just above the level of the lancet openings in its walls.[46] Indeed, most contemporary allusions to the unrestored crossing refer to it simply as 'the dome'.

The plan records that the walls of the crossing, above eaves level, were reduced in thickness from 5 ft to 3 ft, but whether the resultant offset (which still exists) was an original features, or was introduced subsequently, is unknown. Substantial parts of the octagonal turrets clearly survived at all four corners of the tower, and those on the north-east and south-west had newel stairs in them; the others may have been either solid or hollow.[47]

The second drawing is by Wren's assistant, William Dickinson, and is dated 8 June 1724. It comprises a sectional elevation of the upper part of the crossing, upon which a new king-post roof had been constructed by Wren. [**32**] He must have regarded this as a short-term measure, since he clearly had more ambitious ideas for the future treatment of the crossing. The domed plaster ceiling is again indicated, but superimposed upon the elevation is an arrangement of three arches, clearly of masonry and evidently indicative of

some kind of vaulted ceiling. This drawing has the appearance of being a proposal to rebuild the crossing piers (see below, p. 32) and to replace the plaster ceiling with a stone vault, as precursors to the eventual erection of a tower and spire. However, it is not easy to reconcile these architects' drawings with an internal view of the quire in *c.* 1700, which clearly shows three of the ribs of an octopartite vault over the crossing, where, at that date, we should expect to see a domical plaster ceiling.[48] [**33**] A simple explanation, which accommodates all the evidence, might be that the ribbed vault was a sixteenth-century creation in timber and plaster, and that this was replaced in the late seventeenth or early eighteenth century with a simple domical ceiling.[49]

What conclusions can be drawn from this disparate and partially conflicting evidence? The late medieval octagonal lantern was destroyed sometime between *c.* 1509 and 1544, leaving *in situ* the base of Henry III's lantern, including substantial parts of its four octagonal corner-turrets. The remains were roofed in an *ad hoc* fashion, as glimpsed in the mid-sixteenth-century drawing. [**29**] The upper part of the crossing now became a windowless box with paired openings into the adjacent roof voids. A certain amount of reconstruction, squaring-off the angles of the octagonal lantern, and integrating the corner-turrets, seems to have taken place in the sixteenth century, making the structure easier to roof. The reduction in thickness of the side walls may have occurred at the same time. The masonry of the box-like top to the crossing extended only as high as the window sills in the present lantern, and the apex of its roof – which must have been pyramidal in form – rose to approximately the same level as the ridges of the adjacent medieval high roofs.

Thus, by the mid-sixteenth century there was no lantern or other structural projection above the ridge-line of main roofs of the Abbey, a fact confirmed by numerous seventeenth- and early eighteenth-century topographical views. However, what these views all failed to record is that the medieval masonry at the corners of the crossing would have protruded at the angles between the four high roofs. It is not surprising that such archaeological detail, which made no significant impact on the overall appearance of the church, was not recorded by most of the topographical artists, who simplified the roof-lines.

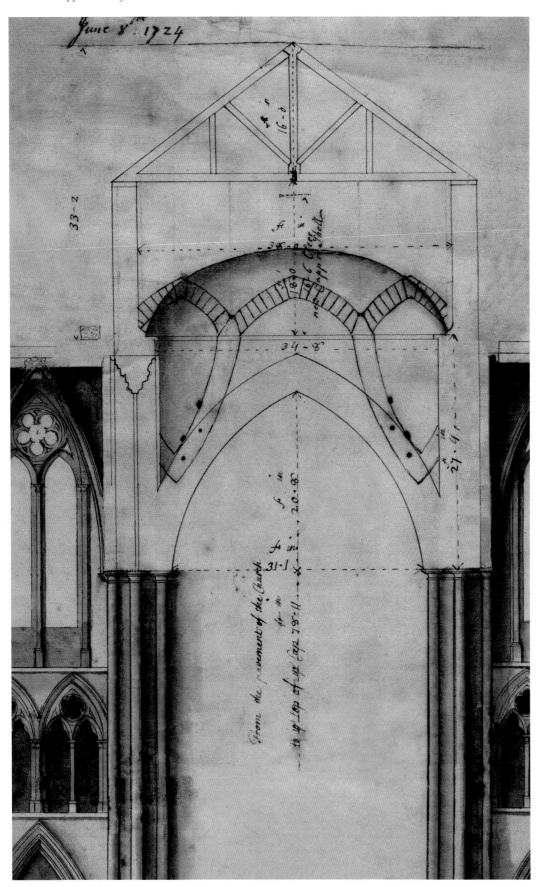

June 8th 1724

32 *Dickinson, 1724. Elevation of the interior of the crossing, showing the Tudor box-like top, with its elliptical ceiling and Wren's new but temporary roof. The proposed reconstruction of the crossing piers and insertion of a stone vault are also shown; these features anticipated the erection of the great tower and spire seen in Figure 34. WAM (P)911*

33 Anonymous, c. 1700. View east in the quire, showing an octopartite vault rising from a string-course immediately above the crossing arches. WA Lib. Coll.

6

Sir Christopher Wren's Ambitious Tower and Spire

Once we reach the eighteenth century, historical records relating to the development of the lantern, both proposed and actual, become more plentiful, although far from complete. Some of the evidence sheds valuable light on earlier vicissitudes too, and this has already been embraced in the previous chapter.

The First Report on the Fabric, 1713

Sir Christopher Wren was appointed Surveyor of the Fabric of Westminster Abbey in 1698. His principal assistant (Under Surveyor) was William Dickinson, who remained briefly in post after Wren's death in 1723. Wren was continuously engaged, *inter alia*, on a comprehensive re-roofing campaign from 1699 to 1718, and in 1713 he reported to Francis Atterbury, the newly installed dean, on the current state of the fabric.[50] He described the works undertaken to date, set out 'what yet remains to finish the necessary repairs', and presented his 'thoughts and designs, in order to [achieve] a proper compleating [*sic*] of what is left imperfect, hoping we may obtain for this the continuation of the Parliamentary assistance'.[51] Given Wren's long association with Westminster, it is unfortunate that the Abbey has only sixteen drawings emanating from his office.[52] Some of these are pertinent to the crossing.

From an early stage in his surveyorship, Wren clearly set his sights upon building an impressive crossing tower and spire, and in 1710 he had a model made in oak and pear wood demonstrating his proposal.[53] [**34**] The model, which cost £30 and stands 2.36 m high, is still extant.[54] It was made to a scale of 4 feet to one inch (*i.e.* 1:48) and thus represents a proposed structure some 372 ft (114 m) high. The tower was square with attached octagonal corner-turrets, and there were two main stages, the upper being a belfry. It had crenellated parapets, and pinnacles at the corners, and from the centre rose a lofty twelve-sided needle-spire, pierced at two levels by lancet openings in every facet.

Referring to the lantern, Wren noted that the construction of a Gothic tower had been started, 'the beginnings of which appear on the corners of the cross', but that it was abandoned 'before it rose so high as the ridge of the roof'. He clearly saw the remnants of Henry III's angle-turrets and incorporated them in his design. Wren added that 'the vault of the quire under it is only lath and plaister, now rotten'. This description refers to the ceiling over the crossing, which was finished as a 'dome' and, as already noted, is shown both on Wren's plan and section of 1715 [**31**], and on Dickinson's section of 1724. [**32**]

Structural Strengthening to Support a Tower

Wren advocated the building of an impressive steeple, first pointing to the problem that

34 Wren, 1710. Timber model of his proposed crossing tower and spire. WA Lib. Coll.

beset the four crossing piers (or pillars, as they were termed): 'it is manifest to the eye that the four innermost pillars of the cross are bended inward considerably, and seem to tend to ruin, and the arches of the second order above are cracked also'. He was referring here to the triforium arcades. He continued, 'lest it should be doubted whether the four pillars below be able to bear a steeple, because they seem a little swayed inward, I have considered how they may be unquestionably secured, so as to support the greatest weight that need be laid upon them; and this after a manner that will add to their shape and beauty'. The bowing of the crossing piers was a result of the lateral thrust exerted on each of them, from two directions, namely by both the main arcades and the triforia. He illustrated the engineering principles with a diagram.[55] Wren attributed the failing to the absence of the intended central tower, the dead-weight of which, he argued, would have anchored the piers and prevented their bowing. This is the same principle as applies to the design of flying buttresses, where masonry is piled, as a counterpoise, on top of a buttress that has to take the lateral thrust from a flier.

Wren also noted with interest the presence of wrought iron tie-bars at capital level in the main arcades, the purpose of which was to connect all the piers to one another and also to the outer walls of the aisles. [35, 72] He concluded that the function of the bars adjacent to the crossing was to restrain the arches from spreading and applying a lateral thrust to the crossing piers, noting that the medieval master mason, 'tied these arches every way with iron', so that 'this might serve the turn till he built the tower to make all secure, which is not done to this day'.

Wren then made the interesting observation that 'these irons which were hooked on from pillar to pillar have been stolen away; and this is the reason of the four [crossing] pillars being bent inward, and the walls above cracked'. Today, all the tie-bars linked to the crossing piers are present, which raises the question as to whether some had been removed and were replaced either by Wren or by one of his successors. There is no evidence to suggest that Wren did any work in the crossing, and this fell to Hawksmoor (p. 53).[56] Moreover, although the expression 'stolen away' might seem to imply that the bars had been removed altogether, that was almost certainly not the case. Wren used the term in the now-archaic sense of implying movement by stealth. In other words, he observed that the hooks onto which the eyes of the tie-bars were threaded had gradually been pulled away from their anchorages in the capitals: several inches of movement would have been possible before the

35 Iron tie-bars linking the capitals of the arcade piers to one another, and to the aisle walls. Note the right-hand end of the bar in the foreground retains its original fixing (sandwiched between the abacus and capital), whereas the left-hand end has been refixed to a stirrup attached to the arch moulding above the abacus. View north-west from the south transept. Author

36 Wren, 1715. Ground plan of the crossing, showing a proposal to enlarge the four piers and their bases. South is at the top. Bodleian Library, Oxford: Gough Mss. Wren Society 1934

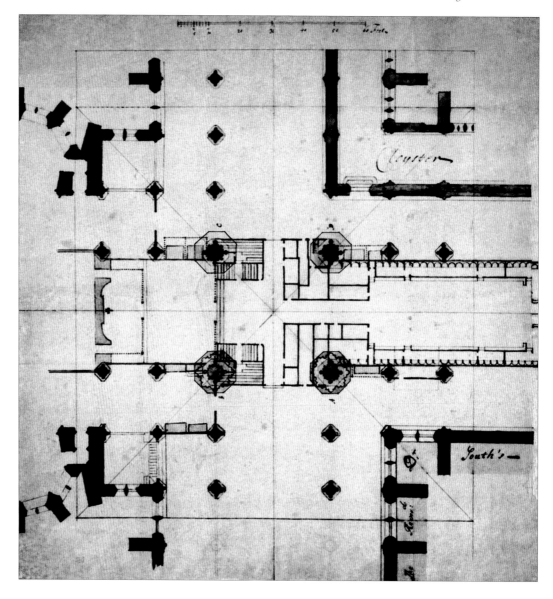

hooks were completely withdrawn, allowing the bars to fall. There is nothing to suggest that happened.

Wren devised a scheme for restoring strength to the crossing piers, and made a model to demonstrate how this was to be achieved. He did not describe the method in his report, and the model has not survived, but we know that the solution was to be 'after a manner that will add to their shape and beauty'. We can, however, reconstruct Wren's proposal in respect of the piers since a surviving plan shows that his solution involved encasing the bowed piers inside new and much larger ones which would of course be plumb.[57] His drawing shows that he intended to enlarge the octagonal plinths of the piers from 8½

ft (2.6 m) to 12 ft (3.7 m), and to simplify the mouldings of the shafts, giving them a late medieval profile. [36, 37] As Wren cautioned, 'this must be first done, otherwise the addition of weight upon that which is already crooked and infirm will make it more so'. Thankfully, the work was never carried out: if it had, the elegant and skilful articulation of the crossing with the four arms of Henry III's church would have been wrecked.

The crossing piers were plumbed by Hawksmoor in June 1724 and a note appended to Wren's earlier drawing (1715). Their height was given as 78 ft 10¾ ins (24.04 m), from the pavement to the top of the capitals.[58] The amounts by which they were out of upright were recorded,[59] but unfortunately it was not

A

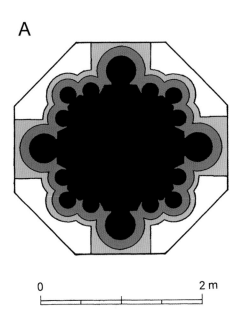

0   2 m

B

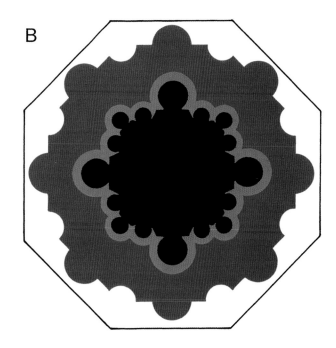

noted which face of the pier was measured, there being three possibilities for each. The measurements appear to relate to the deviation from verticality between the top and bottom of each pier, and are not a record of the amount by which they bowed in the middle region. Structural issues will be further explored in the next chapter (p. 57).

Once the piers had been secured, Wren proposed to build a tower 'according to the original intention of the architect. … In my opinion the tower should be continued to at least as much in height above the roof as it is in breadth' (*i.e.* a minimum of 44 ft, or 13.4 m), adding that 'if a spire be added to it, it will give proper grace to the whole fabric, and the West-end of the City, which seems to want it'. He insisted that he would 'strictly adhere' to the Gothic style: 'to deviate … would be to run into a disagreeable mixture, which no person of a good taste could relish'.[60] The timber model, which represented Wren's proposal, owed much to the central tower and spire of Salisbury Cathedral. However, he added the comment, 'I have varied a little from the usual form, in giving twelve sides to the spire instead of eight'.[61] Wren evidently considered a number of possibilities for detailing the tower and spire, and a plan dated 1715 (drawn to the same scale as the model) shows both the octagonal and dodecagonal options.[62] The scheme included detached octagonal stair-

turrets at the four corners of the tower. [31] Interestingly, Wren's assistant titled the drawing 'plan and section for the "light shell" described in Sir Chr. Wren's report of 1713'. Given that a major strengthening of the crossing piers was envisaged, the term 'light shell' undoubtedly relates to the structure's function as a lantern, and not to its weight.

It may be noted, *en passant*, that the phenomenon of bowed crossing piers is by no means unique to Westminster, and it is found in a number of other churches where the piers are tall and slender: *e.g.* Amiens Cathedral. There too the lofty crossing does not (now) support a masonry tower which would have provided a dead-load: the original termination is unknown, but since the early sixteenth century the crossing has been topped with a relatively lightweight *flèche*. [6]

William Dickinson's Contribution

Wren's ambitious scheme languished, presumably for lack of funds, but also perhaps on account of declining energy in his final years: he died in 1723, aged 90. His successor as Surveyor of the Fabric was Nicholas Hawksmoor, who adopted not only many of Wren's ideas, but also retained his assistant William Dickinson (Under Surveyor, 1711–25). Several drawings relating to the crossing in the hand of the latter have survived, demonstrating that completing the

37 A. Plan of a thirteenth-century crossing pier and its octagonal plinth, as existing. B. Plan showing Wren's proposal to encase the medieval pier inside a new and much larger one. Author

lantern tower was once again a matter receiving serious consideration. While still working for his old master, Dickinson prepared drawings for at least three schemes: the first two envisaged the erection of a 95-ft (29 m) high square central tower with octagonal corner-turrets and crenellations. Various further options involving a soaring spire and a dome were presented. The third scheme allowed for raising the tower more modestly and surmounting it with a domed lantern and cupola.

Scheme 1

Dickinson's first scheme is dated 1722, and has much in common with Wren's model. It shows a conventional embattled and pinnacled tower with octagonal corner-turrets. [**38**, **39**] Options for the treatment of the fenestration and parapets are shown to left and right. The tower is also fitted with a tall needle-spire with lucarnes, taking the overall height to 280 ft (85 m). The dodecagonal spire is divided into three registers by decorative bands which are fussy and fragment its outline.[63]

Scheme 2

This is also dated 1722, and five basic versions were drawn, together with various sub-options. The options were presented by arranging a series of flaps on the drawing which could be opened to reveal further variants.[64]

Version (i) shows a conventional square tower with crenellations, octagonal angle-turrets and pinnacles, but no spire; it had arcading and lancet windows around the lower two stages, all in the Early English style, and tall, ogival-headed windows in the uppermost stage, based on fourteenth-century prototypes. [**40**] Drawn

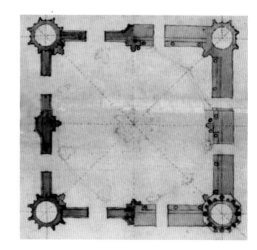

40 (far left) Dickinson, 1722. Scheme 2, version (i): a crossing tower of three stages with a parapet and pinnacles, but without a spire or dome. WAM (P)909

41 (left) Dickinson, 1722. Scheme 2, version (ia): option for a dome and spirelet instead of a crenellated parapet. WAM (P)909

It represents a development of the dome shown in (ia). All this is overlaid on the fainter outline of a tall, plain needle-spire with twelve facets. [42] Two further variations (versions iia and iib) show minor differences to the lantern and cupola.[66]

Scheme 3

The third scheme is dated 1722 and is more restrained. This envisaged an octagonal drum-like lantern with two tiers of fenestration, modest pinnacles and a lead-covered dome pierced by small windows.[67] [43] It had semi-detached octagonal stair-turrets at the corners of the tower, rising only to roof-ridge height. What is undoubtedly the plan relating to this scheme is attached to the survey drawing of 8 June 1724, and separately bears the same date.[68]

alongside this, on a separately attached sheet (not a flap), is an alternative version (ia) for topping the tower with a twelve-sided, ribbed and crocketed lantern-dome surmounted by a spirelet, and having small pinnacles at the four corners. It comprises a mixture of Gothic and classical detail, the latter including acorn and pineapple finials.[65] [41]

Version (ii) shows the same tower surmounted by a dodecagonal lantern with a ribbed lead dome, and a cupola with a spirelet.

42 (right) Dickinson,
1722. Scheme 2, version
(ii): a crossing tower with
a lead dome (a variation
on Figure 39) and
spirelet. A needle-spire is
shown as an alternative
in the background.
WAM (P)909

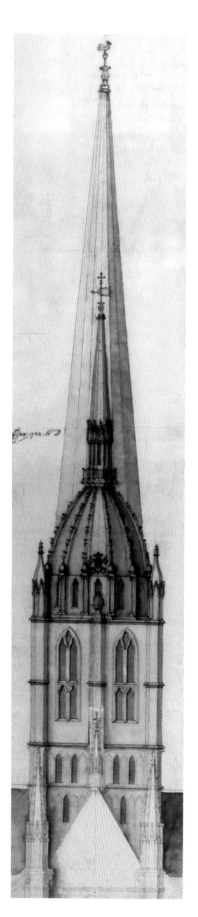

43 (far right) Dickinson,
1722. Scheme 3: an
octagonal drum-shaped
lantern tower and lead
dome over the crossing.
WAM (P)908

[44] The plan is plainly derivative from Wren's drawing of 1715 (p. 25). [31]

Scheme 4

An undated ink drawing, evidently by Dickinson, shows in meticulous detail his final scheme (prepared for Wren) for restoring the north transept gable and, above it, faintly drawn in pencil, is an equally detailed elevation of the proposed crossing tower.[69] It is square in plan, has two stages with windows (the upper a belfry), crenellated parapets and ornate pinnacles. [45] The drawing, which bears close comparison with Figure 38, may represent Dickinson's earliest proposal for the lantern tower.

Although a good deal of effort obviously went into formulating these proposals, nothing materialized because Dickinson died in 1725. John James was appointed to succeed him as Under Surveyor,[70] eventually becoming Surveyor of the Fabric himself in 1736. It is difficult to draw clear lines of demarcation between the various proposals advanced by Wren, Dickinson and Hawksmoor. Dickinson was in the employ of Wren by 1696, and worked up schemes for him at Westminster, introducing his own proposals in the early 1720s. Hawksmoor, who had joined Wren's office in *c.* 1680, borrowed from both men, merging their ideas with his own; he also worked with Sir John Vanbrugh from the late 1690s, adding another source of inspiration to his design repertoire.

Finally, a common source of confusion needs explanation: the two views of Westminster Abbey engraved by Paul Fourdrinier in 1737, purporting to show the spire 'as designed by Sir Christopher Wren', bear no resemblance to the 1710 model, or to any drawings known to have emanated from Wren's office. Allusion to Wren is largely honorific, and acknowledges the fact that he was the originator of the proposal to

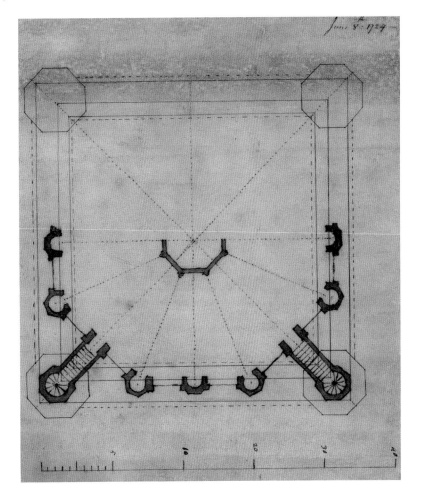

erect a tower and spire over the crossing. It was Hawksmoor who developed the final scheme for completing not only the lantern but also the western towers. The engravings have been reproduced many times, and the supposed connection with Wren much rehearsed. One of the views is by the hand of John James, and was engraved in the year following Hawksmoor's death.[71] [84] Similarly, the drawing showing the western towers and lantern spire, published by William Maitland in 1739, bore a misleading legend, attributing the design to Wren.[72]

44 Dickinson, 1724. Plan of the proposed octagonal lantern and spire illustrated in Figure 41. The semi-detached octagonal corner-turrets shown here are smaller than the medieval originals. The larger octagons drawn in outline at the corners represent the plinths of the crossing piers at church floor level. WAM (P)911

45 *Dickinson (attributed), c. 1720. The north transept gable is shown as it was restored by Dickinson, and added in pencil is his scheme 4 for a substantial crossing tower with a belfry but no spire. WAM (P)902*

7

Begun, but still Incomplete: Nicholas Hawksmoor's Crossing Tower and Spire

Nicholas Hawksmoor was appointed as the next Surveyor of the Fabric in 1723, and held the post until he died in 1736. In the mid-1720s the clear goal in the minds of both Hawksmoor and the Dean and Chapter was to crown the crossing with a tower or lantern of some sort, and to complete the twin western towers.[73] While the concept enjoyed both Parliamentary and public support, arriving at a scheme which satisfied all parties required patience and the tabling of numerous options. The House of Commons was still voting funds annually for 'repairing and completing' Westminster Abbey, although there appear to have been constant financial difficulties.[74] More drawings were produced, representing at least six schemes, with a variety of further sub-options for detailing the crossing although, interestingly, most of these did not include a tall Gothic tower or a soaring spire, as envisaged by Wren and Dickinson, but tended to favour a domed lantern and cupola. Several of Hawksmoor's schemes represent only minor reworkings of earlier proposals by Wren and Dickinson. Ironically, in his final scheme Hawksmoor once again embraced the idea of a tower and spire over the crossing, and work to this end was commenced. But for an accident of history, that would have been completed by 1730.

Hawksmoor's Surveyorship was dominated by the subject of towers at Westminster Abbey, but only a small fraction of the documentation that must have been produced over the 13-year period has survived. Several drawings by

Hawksmoor had long been preserved amongst the Abbey's muniments, and a few others relating to towers were known elsewhere, but they did not tell a coherent story. However, in 1993 fresh light was shed on the proposals of the 1720s when a cache of twenty hitherto unknown drawings was found in the attic of a country house, and were purchased on behalf of the Abbey.[75] All are considered together here.

The Hawksmoor Drawings

Scheme 1

What is almost certainly the earliest of Hawksmoor's schemes is preserved in a sectional elevation of the crossing.[76] [46] It shows the crossing piers in their original form, not enlarged but carrying a square lantern tower of two stages with octagonal corner-turrets, crenellations and pinnacles. The tower in turn supports a tall dodecagonal spire of three stages, with decorative bands and lucarnes in the cardinal faces only. The legend records that the complete structure would stand to a height of 400 ft (122 m) above pavement level in the quire. The design was clearly inspired by Wren's model of 1710, while at the same time being derivative from Dickinson's scheme 1, dated 1722. [38]

Scheme 2

This drawing is also undated, but must again be attributable to 1723–24.[77] Several options are

46 (right) Hawksmoor, c. 1723–24. Scheme 1: a crossing tower of two stages, with a parapet, pinnacles and a three-stage spire. The total height was to be 400 feet. WAM (P)913

47 (far right) Hawksmoor, c. 1723–24. Scheme 2, version (i): a square crossing tower of three stages, with corner-turrets, a crenellated parapet and pinnacles. WAM (P)912

presented on paper flaps. In version (i) it shows a spire-less tower closely similar to that seen in scheme 1, but now of three fenestrated stages instead of two. [47] In version (ii), the same tower is topped by a two-stage octagonal cupola with windows, the construction evidently being of timber and lead. [48] Two further variations exist, showing the lantern finished, first with a short spirelet (version iii), and then with a taller one (version iv). [49]

Scheme 3

A drawing, dated 1724, shows a plain square base (up to ridge-level), surmounted by an octagonal lantern with paired lights in the four cardinal faces and canopied statue niches applied in the angled sides. [50] The lantern was

48 (far left) Hawksmoor, c. 1723–24. Scheme 2, version (ii): the same tower as in Figure 47, surmounted by a two-stage, lead-covered cupola with an ogival base. WAM (P)912

49 (left) Hawksmoor, c. 1723–24. Scheme 2, version (iii): the same tower and cupola as in Figure 47, but this time finished with a short spirelet. Alongside, on a flap, is an alternative for a taller spirelet (version (iv)). WAM (P)912

roofed with an ogival lead dome. This was the simplest of Hawksmoor's schemes, involving the construction of a much lower tower than had previously been envisaged. An addition was made to the drawing, dated 1731, in the form of a plan showing freestanding octagonal stair-turrets in place of the statue niches.[78] A second drawing relating to this scheme comprises a half-section along the length of the church, looking south and showing how

Hawksmoor proposed to treat the interior of the crossing and lantern.[79] [51]

Following Wren's proposal (p. 32), the main piers have been increased in size, and the capitals now support low semicircular arches, surmounted by crocketed canopies of ogival form.[80] Above is a pointed relieving arch which does not correspond to the existing Gothic crossing arch, implying that the latter was to be destroyed and replaced. At eaves level the

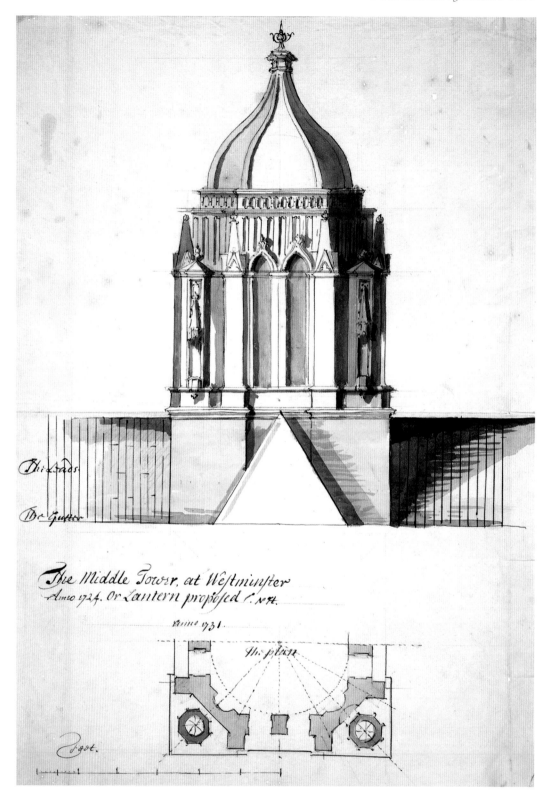

thickness of the tower wall has been reduced and pierced by a large arch containing a triplet of smaller pointed arches, opening into the void of the high roof beyond. Just above ridge-level is the junction between the square tower and the octagonal lantern, the angled faces of which are carried on shell-shaped squinches. Internally the lantern is finished with

51 Hawksmoor, 1724. Scheme 3: south-facing section through the proposed tower and lantern, showing the proposed treatment of the interior of the crossing. A plan of the upper stage of the lantern is also included. WAM (P)910

a hemispherical dome, the crown of which stands 185 ft (56.5 m) above floor level.

Scheme 4

Another drawing, which probably dates from 1724, shows the entire north elevation of the Abbey 'with ye west towers and the middle lantern as intended'. Again, by affixing a series of flaps, Hawksmoor offered three possible versions of the proposed lantern tower.[81] Version (i) shows a low, square tower finished with a cornice and parapet just above ridge level. Rising behind that is a large onion-shaped dome with crocketed ribs, oval *oculi* and a ball-finial surmounted by a cross. [52] Visually, the whole composition is heavy and

squat. In version (ii) Hawksmoor attempted to alleviate this effect by attenuating the onion-shaped dome and adding a crocketed collar and stem below the ball-finial. [53] The result completely overwhelmed the diminutive tower upon which it was placed. So, Hawksmoor attempted version (iii), in which he first raised the square tower by adding a blind-panelled stage; then came a buttressed octagonal stage with windows in the cardinal faces and capped staircases against the others; on top of that he added a short, octagonal stage with large quatrefoiled openings in each face, a crenellated parapet and spindly pinnacles; finally, the whole composition was completed with a highly ornate lead dome and finial. [54] For all its

*52 Hawksmoor,
c. 1724. Scheme 4,
version (i): the crossing
does not rise above ridge
level, and is finished
with a parapet and
squat dome. WAM,
Hawksmoor no. 4*

*53 Hawksmoor,
c. 1724. Scheme 4,
version (ii): this has
the same parapet as in
Figure 52, but a more
attenuated dome. WAM,
Hawksmoor no. 4*

stylistic idiosyncrasies, the last is visually the most satisfactory.

Schemes 5 and 6

Hawksmoor prepared two elevations of the north side of the Abbey, to show how it might look if it were completely remodelled as a quasi-classical structure, while retaining Gothic tracery in the windows.[82] These undated designs owe not a little to St Paul's Cathedral and to All Souls' College, Oxford, upon both of which Hawksmoor had previously been engaged. His designs of 1720 for the cloister and west gate at All Souls are especially relevant.[83] The two schemes show the lantern tower as a massive, squat structure with an ogival dome set between four square turrets. [**55, 56**] The resemblance of the central tower to a mosque has also been noted.[84]

These schemes were radically different from all others in that they involved the enlargement of the crossing to take in the adjacent bay on all sides. To achieve this would have required a drastic reconstruction of the centre of the church.

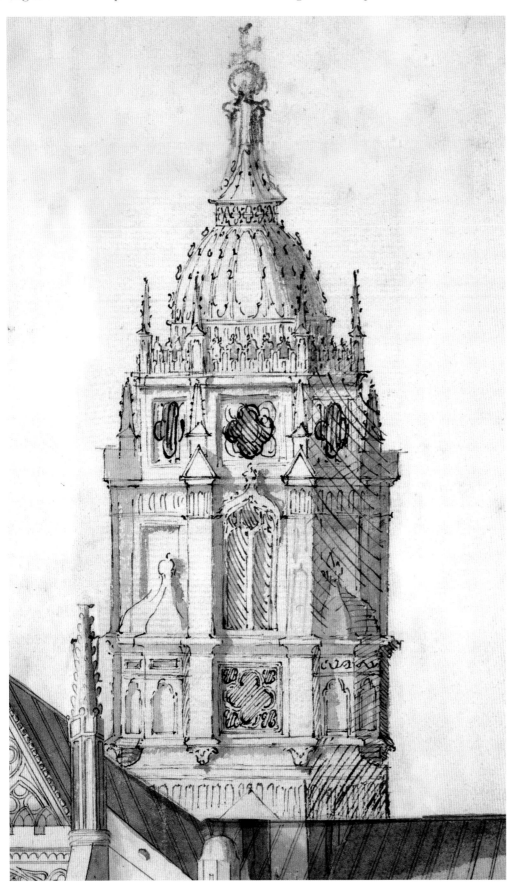

*54 Hawksmoor,
c. 1724. Scheme 4,
version (iii): the crossing
is topped by a highly
ornate octagonal lantern
and dome. WAM,
Hawksmoor no. 4*

Repairing the Damaged Medieval Crossing

In April 1724, the newly appointed Hawksmoor erected a scaffold inside the crossing, 'to examine the condition of the sealing of the middle tower which appears ruinous, and dangerous to be under, and to see what condition the four large leggs of the said tower are now in'.[85] On 8 June 1724, Dickinson (who was now employed in Hawksmoor's office) prepared a sectional elevation drawing with dimensions. It appears to have been taken on the north–south axis, and shows a plain, low tower with the walls above the crossing arches reduced in thickness, a simple ridged roof without a parapet, and a shallow domed ceiling.[86] [32] Superficially, this might be taken to represent a lightweight, minimalist solution to enclosing the crossing, but it is undoubtedly a record drawing, not a proposal. As already observed, it can be identified as a section through the sixteenth-century boxed-in top of the crossing (p. 26).[87]

Dismantling the upper part of the crossing evidently began straightaway, since Edward Stanton, the mason, submitted a bill for work done by him between June and Michaelmas 1724, 'taking down the stone walls of the middle tower or dome, and placing by all the good and useful stone there taken down'.[88] In April 1725 an estimate was prepared for 'finishing the doome to the ridge of the roof of the church & repairing the 4 great arches and vaulting from the pillars'. At the same time, Hawksmoor was also instructed to inspect 'the spandrills and arches adjoining to the dome [to] make a report what more it will be absolutely necessary to take down'.[89] This refers principally to the triforium arcades adjacent to the crossing, the fractured condition of which had already been noted by Wren in 1713. Some repair must also have been necessary at clearstorey level, since this will have been affected by structural movement too.

For next three years workmen were employed in the crossing, dismantling and reconstructing the masonry at the base of the tower. In May 1725, they were authorized to rebuild only up to the level of the 'battlement of the church, provided the old stones that were taken down from the said dome will be sufficient for that purpose … and to desist from going so far if the old stone will not hold out to do it'.[90] This

confirms that there was no masonry tower rising up to or beyond ridge level, otherwise there would not have been a shortage of building stone. We may therefore deduce that Stanton's men had removed the sixteenth-century boxing of the top of the lantern, and the plaster dome inside; they must also have dismantled any masonry that remained of the former octagonal lantern base and its corner supports, in order to access and repair the fractured crossing arches. That having been done, they began to build up the walls again with what little stone was available for reuse. The level from which the reconstruction took place is plainly visible in the masonry today, as well as being marked on Hawksmoor's elevation drawing. [15, 57, 58, 59]

Hawksmoor's Model of the Crossing

In April 1726 Hawksmoor was authorized to carry the reconstruction up to the next level, namely 'to the top of the old roof … according to [the] model now laid before the Committee'.[91] Mention of a model calls to mind a series of fragments of limestone models, now in the Westminster Abbey Collection. Some of these fragments are identifiable as relating to the crossing. A reference to the commissioning

57 Masonry in the spandrels above the main arches at the north-west angle of the crossing. The small blocks in the lower area are part of Henry III's work, while everything above belongs to Hawksmoor's rebuild (cf. Figs 15 and 59). Author

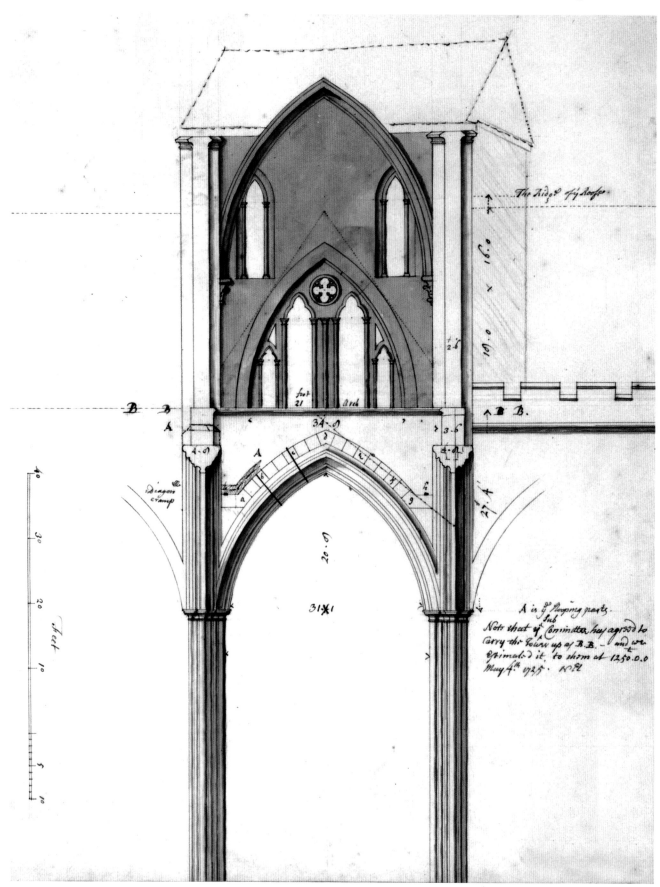

of a model of proposed works in the crossing is preserved in the muniments: in September 1724, Edward Stanton, the mason who dismantled the old lantern, billed the Abbey for 'modelling a design according to Mr Hawksmoor's directions for the finishing of the said middle tower or dome'. His charges included 'for 10.0 cub. of freestone for the model at 2*s*. 1*d*. per foot – £1 0*s*. 10*d*.' This model must have been quite substantial for ten cubic feet of limestone to have been used in its making. Constructed at a scale of 4 feet

to one inch (*i.e.* 1:48), the quantity of stone purchased would have been ample to make a model of a tower and spire representing a height of three hundred feet, or more. The situation is however complicated by the fact that there were interchangeable components, so that the model could be reassembled to show several variations on the basic proposal.

Only a few fragments of Hawksmoor's model survive today, and these relate to the easternmost bay of the nave vault, the north-west crossing pier, the lantern and the proposed

60 Hawksmoor's stone model, 1724: component A. North-west corner of the crossing, showing the capital and springing of the north and west arches and part of the vault of the easternmost bay of the nave. On the far right is the beginning of the first bay of the north transept clearstorey. WA Lib. Coll.

vaulted ceiling ('dome') over the crossing itself.[92] In all, five components of the model partially survive, and three of them appear to represent alternative treatments of the lantern stage. To some extent they complement the extant drawings (p. 39). The model did not encompass the entire tower and lantern, from the floor upwards, but began just below the springing of the crossing arches. Also, the tower may only have been represented by the western half-section. The material used for the model is fine-grained cream limestone. Architects' models in stone are much rarer than those in timber, and these fragments are thus an important survival.[93]

Components A and B
These two adjoining pieces are from the lowest part of the model and comprise the easternmost bay of the nave vault, together with the capital of the north-west crossing pier and parts of the two great arches springing from it; also included is a small fragment of the first bay of the north transept. The crossing pier is shown in its thirteenth-century form, and not the enlarged version proposed by Wren and Hawksmoor. [60]

Component C
Several non-adjoining fragments evidently belong to a model of the lower part of an octagonal lantern, with pairs of pointed windows in each face. [61, 62] The window heads are surmounted by ogival canopies

61 (right) Hawksmoor's stone model, 1724: component C. Reconstruction of part of the octagonal lantern stage with a pair of windows in the cardinal face and freestanding corner-turrets with fliers adjacent to the diagonal faces. WA Lib. Coll.

62 (far right) Hawksmoor's stone model, 1724: component C. Reconstruction of part of the octagonal lantern stage (as in Fig. 61), showing a window with a crocketed ogee-headed canopy. WA Lib. Coll.

embellished with crockets and poppyhead finials. Two freestanding octagonal corner-turrets survive, complete with evidence at their bases for roofed link-structures which would have facilitated access from the top of the turret-stair into the base of the lantern. Higher up on each turret is a flier which provided a supporting link between the lantern and the turret. This section of the model must have stood directly on top of the square basement stage of the crossing tower, the octagonal turrets rising from the four corners and being supported from below by corbelling or squinch arches.[94] The design possibly relates to one of the Wren-Dickinson plans, or a derivative. [**31**, **44**]

Component D

This half-section represents a high-domed vault contained within the upper stage of an octagonal lantern, above the windows. [**63**] The octopartite ribbed vault is intact, and has a bell manhole or *oculus* at the centre. Externally, the model has no elaboration, although there are hints of setting-out lines for blind tracery on one of the faces.

Component E

This is another half-section of the upper part of a square lantern tower. [**64**] It represents the vaulted stage above the lantern windows, and shows that there was a ribbed vault of twelve compartments, contained inside a square tower with attached octagonal turrets at the angles.

The vault itself has been broken away and only the springings of the ribs survive. The exterior is blank. On the top edge of this section of model are some lightly scored setting-out lines relating to the construction; they also show that there was to be a newel stair in one of the turrets.[95]

Construction of the New Lantern Tower Begins

Even though we lack explicit written evidence detailing the conclusion that had been reached regarding the treatment of the lantern tower, the important point to note is that a firm decision must have been made by May 1725. Rebuilding of the lower stage of the tower could not have begun until it was known what kind of superstructure it had eventually to support (see further, p. 56). It was not necessary for every detail of the upper stages of the lantern to have been decided upon at this point, but the erection of its 'basement' (as Hawksmoor referred to it) would prescribe the general form hereafter.

The construction of the tower base in Portland stone then went ahead in accordance with a surviving drawing dated 4 May 1725.[96] This is an east–west sectional elevation through the crossing, showing a squat and obviously unfinished lantern tower, surmounted by a temporary, gabled roof. [**58**] The style is firmly thirteenth century. Just above the apices of the crossing arches the masonry was reduced in thickness from 5 ft to 3 ft (1.5 m to 0.9 m), at the level defined internally by a broad offset and string-course, and externally by two steps.

63 (left) Hawksmoor's stone model, 1724: component D. Half-section of a rib-vault above an octagonal lantern. This could have fitted on top of component C, except that the latter has pilasters at the angles. WA Lib. Coll.

64 (below) Hawksmoor's stone model, 1724: component E. Half-section of a square tower with octagonal corner-turrets, containing a rib-vault above the lantern stage. WA Lib. Coll.

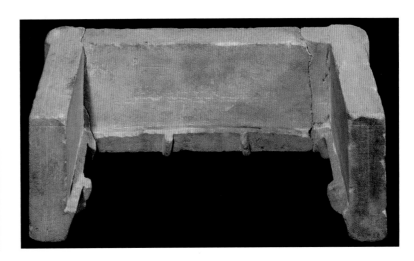

65 *Hawksmoor's north-west angle-turret of the lantern tower, containing a newel staircase which incorporates some medieval masonry in situ. Author*

[**14, 15**] This is the foundation off which the basement stage of the tower was built. Each wall of the tower was pierced by a large opening taking the form of a two-centred arch, the purpose of which was undoubtedly to reduce the superincumbent weight of the tower on the crossing piers. The openings communicated with the voids of the adjacent high roofs. The drawing shows a single bay of traceried arcading within each aperture, the components of which comprise four trefoil-headed arches surmounted by a pierced quatrefoil. [**59**] The design is an adaptation of Henry III's triforium arcade. Above each opening is a pair of lancet windows flanking the apex of the high roof. The section drawing also reveals that the ceiling of the crossing was to be vaulted. The external angles of the tower

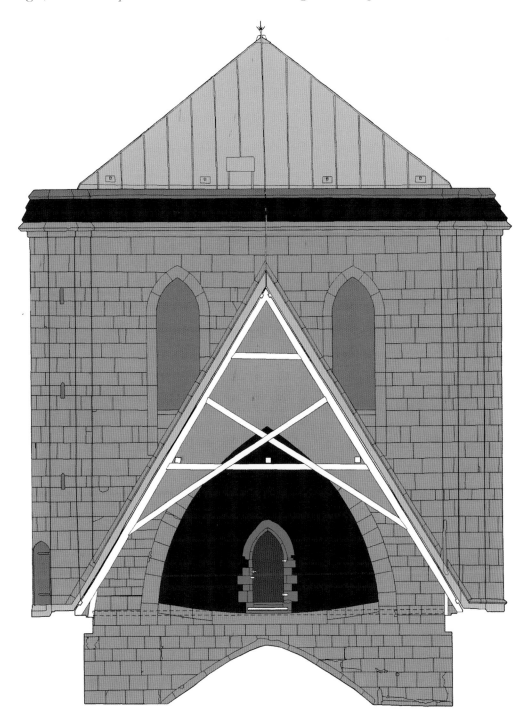

66 External east elevation of Hawksmoor's lantern tower, including the area enclosed within the presbytery roof. Key: orange, Hawksmoor; maroon, Wyatt; blue, Scott; green, modern. The Downland Partnership and author

were clasped by polygonal turrets. As we have seen, these were not only on the sites of their medieval predecessors, but also incorporated some original masonry (p. 12).

Nearly all of the above appears to have been built in 1726–27, since substantial components of what is shown in the drawing are still present in the fabric today, including the octagonal corner-turrets. [**65, 66**] One element is however missing: there is no arcading in the large openings, and later references and illustrations confirm that it was never installed (p. 49). Inside the tower, the archaeological evidence is clear: while the four great arches of the crossing are thirteenth century, albeit repaired, the spandrels flanking them (and meeting at the corners of the tower) contain medieval masonry for less than half their height, the remainder

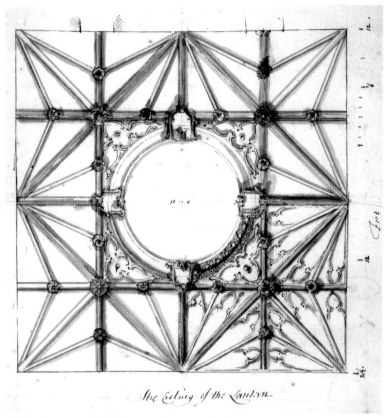

67 Hawksmoor, c. 1725. Plan of the proposed ceiling vault for the lantern. This could be constructed in either stone or plaster. WAM, Hawksmoor no. 10

having been rebuilt in much larger blocks by Hawksmoor. [15, 57]

Hawksmoor designed an ornate, vaulted ceiling for the lantern, and he provided the Dean and Chapter with two estimates: one to construct it in timber and plaster, and the other in 'stone and chalk'.[97] The former option was cheaper and was duly chosen. The vault sprang from corbels at window sill level and the soffit was attached to a timber frame set just below the temporary roof of the tower. [67, 68] In the centre of the ceiling was a circular aperture 10 ft (3 m) in diameter. The vault was clearly conceived as a permanent feature, and not as a temporary work to be superseded when the tower was eventually raised to its intended full height. The circular aperture could be interpreted as a bell-manhole – in which case a belfry must have been envisaged in the upper stage of the tower, which is improbable – but it is more likely to have been designed as an *oculus*, admitting light from a cupola above. In the event, only a lead roof was ever built above the opening, and thus the aperture was never functional.

As an aside, it is worth observing that none of Hawksmoor's proposals, or those drawn up by any other architect, would have made

68 Hawksmoor, c. 1725. Sectional elevation of the proposed ceiling vault for the lantern shown in Figure 67. WAM, Hawksmoor no. 11

an appreciable difference to the volume of light at floor level in the crossing. The lantern is so high above the pavement, relative to its plan-dimensions, that there could be no expectation that shafts of sunlight would beam down upon the monarch during the coronation ceremony. The lantern must always have been regarded as a high-level, light-filled feature upon which to gaze in wonderment from below, and not as a significant source of downward illumination.

Work Stops for the Coronation, 1727

In February 1727 the order was given to install the new timber and plaster 'dome' (*i.e.* Hawksmoor's vaulted ceiling), and to fill up 'the 4 great arches into the roof with timber and boards', also for 'finishing the floor and roof over the dome', and completing the abutments between its walls and the four high roofs.[98] The tower-base was temporarily capped with a low-pitched lead roof without a parapet, and probably included a reinstatement of the pine trusses that had been put on by Wren a few years earlier. Filling the '4 great arches' with timber boarding must also have been regarded as a temporary measure, pending the insertion of the stone arcading that was intended to decorate them, estimates for which had been prepared.[99] Nevertheless, the scaffolding was ordered to be struck by Michaelmas 1727, implying haste to bring the project to a premature conclusion. The imperative for this is not hard to find: King George I had died on 10 June and the coronation of George II and Queen Caroline was scheduled to take place on 11 October. The crossing was, of course, pivotal to the coronation ritual, and it had to be both free from scaffolding and seemly in appearance.[100]

The boarding installed in the four arches had to be decorated in some way, and an undated quotation from William Kent may supply the solution.[101] His proposal, costing £360, was 'For painting, according to the sketches, the four arches in St Peter's, Westminster, and the round in the middle. The figures must be at least twice as big as the life, to be painted upon cloth'. This suggests that allegorical scenes were envisaged. Whether the commission was executed is not recorded, but it seems likely

69 *Dixon, 1784. Detail from an engraving of the nave, looking east. The interior of the lantern tower is glimpsed, and has an arcaded design on the east face. This was not architectural detailing, but was presumably painted on cloth and may have been the work of William Kent. WA Lib. Coll.*

(for possible conflicting evidence, see p. 71). In order to be appreciated, the paintings needed to be lit, and the glazier was instructed to fill the eight lancets in the new lantern base with clear 'Newcastle glass'.[102]

The earliest known view of the interior of Hawksmoor's lantern appears to be an engraving of 1784, showing the staging set up for the public commemoration of G.F. Handel in that year.[103] The lower part of the east face of the lantern is glimpsed, where, directly above the string-course is an arcade of seven rounded arches, alternate ones being subdivided by a mullion and tracery, perhaps to give an illusion of depth, or syncopated arcading.[104] [69] Presumably, this was painted on cloth or canvas, and it is tempting to regard it as William Kent's work, with large allegorical figures filling the undivided arches. The effect would have been of a gallery, with figures looking out.[105] Although of a different order of excellence and robustly classical, one is reminded of the gallery of figures under arches that Kent painted on the king's grand staircase of Kensington Palace, also in the 1720s.[106] Kent's painting would have chimed well with other contemporary decorative elements in the Abbey: the rose window in the north transept, for example, was filled with standing figures designed by Sir James Thornhill in 1722, and the great west window was similarly treated in 1735.

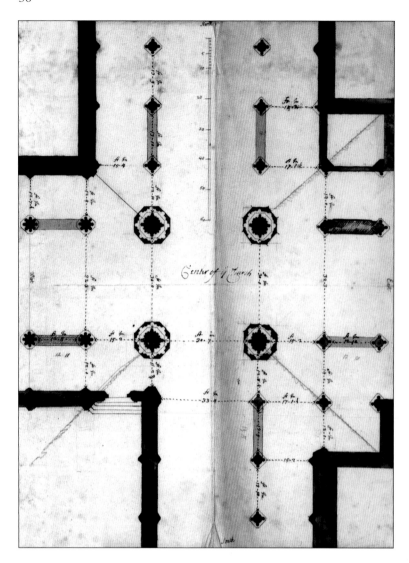

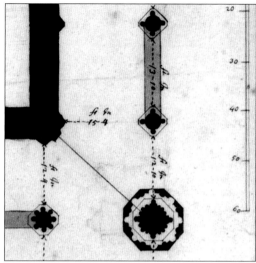

71 Hawksmoor, mid-1720s. Detail from the ground plan of the crossing (Figure 70), showing the north-west pier. It illustrates the proposal to encase the thirteenth-century pier in new masonry, to infill the second bay of the arcades in the nave and transept, and to insert a diagonal iron tie-bar. This is a development of Wren's earlier proposal (Figure 34). Scale of feet. WAM, Hawksmoor no. 20

70 Hawksmoor, mid-1720s. Detail from a ground plan of the nave and transepts, showing the proposal to thicken the crossing piers and infill the second arch of each arcade with masonry. Proposed iron tie-bars at triforium level are also indicated, running diagonally out from the crossing piers. North is at the top. Scale of feet. WAM, Hawksmoor no. 20

Executing Hawksmoor's Final Design

Hawksmoor had evidently adopted one of the Wren–Dickinson designs for the tower, at least in part, since the existing stump has much in common with the lowest stage of the Gothic tower shown in several of Dickinson's drawings. [38, 40, 47] However, nothing more was built, although the intention to continue at a later date cannot be in doubt. Two pieces of evidence are demonstrative. First, the tops of the walls of the lantern are finished, not with a conventional parapet coping, but with a moulded weathering which could have begun life as a string-course of the type that would have separated two structural stages of a tower.[107] Second, there are spiral staircases in the north-west and south-east corner turrets,

which simply end in open air. Having no stair-caps or practicable means of exit on to the roof, they are plainly unfinished and were meant to continue to a higher level.

Had it not been for George II's coronation supervening, the crossing tower project would probably have continued to completion by *c.* 1730. But once the scaffolding was down, the impetus was lost, and attention turned to other fabric matters: initially, this was the erection of a new stone screen between nave and quire, and after that the monumental task of completing the west front was tackled. Notwithstanding, the lantern tower was evidently still under serious consideration, since further drawings were made by Hawksmoor in 1731 and 1732. One has survived, showing the first stage.[108] [58] Drawings for the second lantern stage and spire have been lost, but that they were prepared is confirmed by a payment made to Hawksmoor in May 1732 for 'a design for a spire upon ye centre of the cross[ing] and a section of ye same'.[109]

Raising the lantern tower by another stage, in whatever form it was intended to take, would impose considerable additional loading on the already deformed crossing piers. In 1713, Wren had stressed the need to strengthen the piers

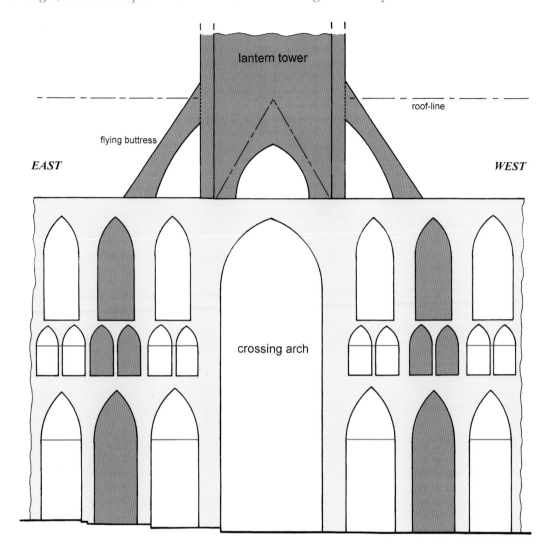

lantern tower

roof-line

flying buttress

EAST

WEST

crossing arch

72 Diagrammatic reconstruction of Hawksmoor's proposal to support the additional loading imposed by a crossing tower by introducing flying buttresses at parapet level. These would create a new load-path through the infilled arcades and windows below, relieving some of the extra weight on the crossing piers. Key: yellow, medieval masonry; orange, Hawksmoor's additions; red, medieval iron tie-bars. Author, after Clive Richardson

before increasing the structural loading (p. 29), and that was no small undertaking. It was the essential next stage, and Hawksmoor was evidently preparing to tackle it. He adopted Wren's idea of encasing the medieval crossing piers inside new, much larger ones, and drew a plan to illustrate the proposal.[110] [**70**, **71**] Unfortunately, it is undated, but his sectional elevation of 1724 illustrates the impact of the scheme on the crossing arches. [**51**] According to the plan, Hawksmoor additionally proposed to infill with masonry the penultimate bay from the crossing in every arcade, so that these were transformed into solid sections of walling. He evidently regarded this as necessary for structural stability, although Wren seemingly did not.

Filling the penultimate bays around the crossing could not provide any support for the bowed piers and can only imply that Hawksmoor was intending to transfer some of the additional loading imposed by the new tower away from the piers altogether, and into the arcades. Although an elevation drawing illustrating how this was to be achieved has not survived, it can be reconstructed from the evidence of the plan. It would have been necessary to infill not only the main arcades, as shown, but also the triforium arches and clearstorey windows directly above. In other words, eight piers of solid masonry would be created from floor to parapet, their function being to carry flying buttresses that would clasp and support the corners of the new tower, creating new load-paths through the fabric. [**72**] The visual effect of enlarging the crossing piers, blocking eight bays of arcading, and infilling the same number of triforium and clearstorey openings would have been devastating, and must have engendered vigorous debate. Unfortunately, no record of this has come down to us.

Notwithstanding the foregoing, it is clear that Hawksmoor designed his lantern tower – the one that was begun – to be as light in weight as possible. Interestingly, none of his schemes show flying buttresses around the central tower, and it would appear that the option was not seriously pursued. Could it be that he was hoping to arrest the deformation of the crossing piers by other means, obviating the need to encase them, and build only a modest lantern? A hint that this may have been the case is found in the minute of the meeting on 10 April 1725, already mentioned, when Hawksmoor was ordered to prepare an estimate for 'finishing the doome to the ridge of the roof' and for '*repairing the 4 great arches and vaulting from the pillars in such a manner as any light ornament may be hereafter carried up upon it without-side*'.[111] Further support for this suggestion is found on the plan, where he shows four tie-bars radiating out from the crossing piers; he doubtless intended to locate these in the triforium, at the point of maximum bowing. The two western ties ran diagonally across the corner bays of the aisles, linking each pier to the external wall at the junction between nave and transept. The eastern ties, on the other hand, not only crossed the corner bays of the aisles, but also extended to the outer angles of the chapels beyond. Hawksmoor later seems to have changed his mind, and struck out three of the four diagonal ties on his plan, leaving only the north-west one, presumably because that was the most seriously deformed corner. [70] In the event, not even that one was installed. Hence, we are led to the conclusion that Hawksmoor decided he could raise a lantern tower over the crossing without strengthening the medieval fabric.

Hawksmoor followed the decision of his predecessors in the mid-sixteenth century not to rebuild the walls of the lantern to their full medieval thickness. He also decided to construct octagonal corner-turrets on the footprint of the originals. [65] Two contain newel stairs, and the others are presumed to be solid (although they are hollow at parapet level). Some of the workmen helpfully left

their marks just inside the south-east turret, including: 'T. Symonds, May 9, 1727', 'T.T. 1727' and 'Ed. Ch'. [73]

Bowed Legs and Rent Fabric

We have already noted that in May 1725 Hawksmoor was instructed to examine and report upon the triforium arcades, which must have been seriously rent by the bowing of the crossing piers. Since the middle sections of those piers had moved inwards towards the centre of the crossing by an average of 10 cm (4 ins), there must have been cracks in the adjacent arches, and in the masonry above and below them, totalling the same. Wren had already drawn attention to the problem in 1713, and Dart reported in 1723 that the bowing of the piers had prevented the proposed erection of a tower and spire in the early sixteenth century (p. 21). There are no visible fractures today, no eye-catching deformation in the arcades, and no obvious evidence for the filling of wide cracks. So, who repaired them, and when? Although the record is silent, we must presume that Hawksmoor was responsible, and the work was most likely carried out hand-in-hand with that on the crossing tower. That would explain why the repairs to the crossing were so protracted, and scaffolding was in place for three years.

It is not easy to determine, without detailed archaeological investigation, precisely what was done in the bays adjacent to the crossing, but three pieces of evidence are worth mentioning. First, the spandrels of the triforium arcades are completely filled with a rectilinear grid of carved surface decoration, but in a few places there are small areas of plain masonry. These can hardly be other than replacements, where the original decorative stone has been lost: the effect is most noticeable in the nave, close to the north-west crossing pier. [74] Second, the spandrel between the first two bays of the main nave arcade on the north contains two vertical

74 North nave triforium (above the quire stalls). Spandrels in the first bay to the west of the crossing, showing where plain ashlar blocks have been substituted for carved masonry during repairs necessitated by movement of the north-west crossing pier. Author

rows of mostly plain ashlar blocks where there should be diapered masonry. [**75**] The third clue concerns the iron tie-bars that link together the main arcade columns, and connect them with the crossing piers. [**35, 72**] Wren mentioned that some of these bars had been 'stolen away' (*i.e.* drawn from their anchorages by being subjected to excessive tension: p. 31), and since that is no longer apparent, we are led to the conclusion that Hawksmoor must have repaired the damage. Whether any of the bars were missing altogether is unknown, but this seems unlikely since a painting of *c.* 1700 confirms that they were still *in situ* to the west of the crossing.[112] [**33**]

However, it is observable that the iron hooks onto which the eyes at the ends of the bars are dropped are not uniform in their placement: most are embedded in the Purbeck marble capitals, but some are set into the abacus (the separate moulding on top of the capital), and in a few instances iron stirrups fitted with hooks have been affixed to the

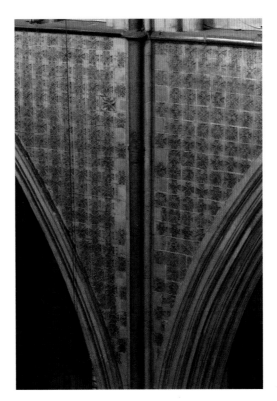

75 North nave arcade (above the quire stalls). Spandrel between the first and second bays to the west of the crossing, showing plain ashlar blocks interspersed amongst the decorative work to either side of the wall-shaft. These blocks probably relate to Hawksmoor's masonry repairs resulting from the displacement of the north-west crossing pier. Author

*76 South transept,
west aisle. Inserted iron
stirrup carrying a hook
for the attachment of a
tie-bar (since removed).
This represents a repair,
probably carried out by
Hawksmoor. Author*

*77 Triorium adjacent to the south-east crossing pier: the first bay of the transept aisle.
The Purbeck marble blocks on which the inner and outer capitals are carved have been
cramped together; also both the tie-bars have been shortened and provided with hooked
ends which engage with secondary eyes inserted into the abacus. Author*

*78 Triorium adjacent to the north-east crossing pier: the first bay of the presbytery aisle.
Detail of the hook-and-eye junction between the outer tie-bar and the arcade capital;
again, this represents a repair. Author*

arch mouldings immediately above the abacus.
[35, 76] The last group plainly represent post-
medieval repairs, and the second group may be
similar. If the tie-bars were still *in situ* when the
crossing piers bowed – and there is no reason
to suspect otherwise – then something had
to give way: either the eyes at the ends of the
bars broke open, or the hooks in the marble
capitals snapped or were torn out. If the latter
happened, the capitals themselves would have
been fractured in the process. Some of the
capitals and abaci display evidence of careful
repair, confirming that failures had occurred.

It was not only the main arcades that were
linked together with iron bars in the thirteenth
century. The much smaller arches of the
triforium openings were similarly tied, although
these did not involve detachable bars secured
with hooks and eyes. Instead, the hooked ends
of the ties were set directly into the tops of the
Purbeck marble capitals before the voussoirs
of the arches were erected upon them. Once
again, any spreading of the arches caused by
the bowing of the crossing piers had to result
in fracture or displacement: either the triforium
capitals would burst and the hooked ends of
the tie-bars would come free, or the capitals
themselves would be pulled bodily out of the
piers into which they were set. Both scenarios
seem to have occurred, but the damage has
been skilfully repaired by Hawksmoor. Several
instances may be observed where a tie-bar that
has broken away from its original anchorage
has been shortened, a new hook formed on its
'free' end, and an eye inserted into the capital
for the reattachment of the hook. Examples
of such repairs made where anchorages had
failed are found in the bays adjacent to both the
north-east and south-east crossing piers. [77,
78] Movement of the north-west pier caused
collateral damage as far as the north side of the
second bay in the transept aisle.

The Crucial Evidence of Pietro Fabris

There is a further source of evidence relating
to Hawksmoor's proposals, which has hitherto
escaped serious consideration. Attributable
to the 1730s are at least three oil paintings by
the Italian-born artist Pietro Fabris, depicting
Westminster Abbey from the north and north-
west. Little is known about the paintings, but
they are likely to have been commissioned to

show how the Abbey might have appeared when restoration and completion of the 'missing' elements had been achieved. Since Parliament was shouldering the cost of 'completing' the Abbey, it is understandable that attractive pictorial representations of the anticipated result were needed to persuade Members of the desirability of making substantial funds available.

We do not know when Fabris was born, but he belonged to the Neapolitan School, was closely associated with Sir William Hamilton, and had a strong interest in England; his *floruit* is generally cited as *c.* 1756–79, solely on the basis of his dated paintings.[113] However, Fabris's Westminster commissions must have come much earlier in his career, since the paintings are datable to the 1730s on internal evidence.

1. A view of the Abbey from the north, showing the line of domestic buildings that extended alongside the nave, and others masking the eastern ambulatory.[114] **[79, 80]** The decision to demolish these was made in 1739, and they were down by the following year. Fabris shows the western towers completed according to Hawksmoor's design, but with the addition of short spires. The lantern tower has a square basement with an overhanging cornice; the next stage comprises an octagonal lantern emerging from a square plinth course. The cardinal faces have Gothic windows with ogival heads, flanked by buttresses with classical detailing. Stair caps abut the diagonal faces. Above is an unbuttressed octagonal stage with an ornate parapet and quatrefoil openings in each face; this supports a lead-covered dome and finial. It is unmistakably Hawksmoor's lantern, shown in his scheme 4, version (iii). **[54]**

2. This depicts the Abbey from the north-west.[115] **[81, 82]** Again, the domestic buildings that obscured much of its northern façade are present, but because the dominant feature of the painting is the north-west tower, the artist has omitted some of the intrusive structures and reduced the height of another by removing the uppermost storey. Had he included these buildings they would have overwhelmed the foreground and seriously detracted from the essential message

that it was trying to convey. Indeed, the excision of some buildings may have been a deliberate attempt to demonstrate how much the north-western aspect of the Abbey would be improved if they were demolished. The painting thereby carries a subtle message. In this view, the north-west tower is shown with less height in the belfry stage, the spire is shorter, and the corner pinnacles are stumpy pyramids. The crossing tower has similar proportions to that in the previous painting, but is more overtly classical, although still retaining some Gothic detailing. The basement and principal stages are both square, and only the cupola and its surrounding parapet are octagonal. We do not have Hawksmoor's drawing corresponding with the lantern in this painting, and it has presumably been lost.

3. Lost too is Fabris's third painting, which is the most important of the trio for our enquiry. It was sold at auction in 1972, and is known today only through a single monochrome photograph which was taken at the time.[116] **[83]** The view is essentially the same as that in the first painting, but now the domestic buildings along the north side of the Abbey have all gone. The completed north-west tower is shown almost exactly as it is today, with only minor differences in detail to the panelling on the faces of the buttresses. Fabris also shows the basement stage of the lantern tower precisely as it was built by Hawksmoor in 1725–27. **[65]** The second stage of the proposed tower is square in plan, of squat proportions, and has two-light traceried windows. These would doubtless have been *en suite* with the openings from the tower into the roof voids in the stage below **[59]**: hence, the intended view from inside the crossing would have been architecturally cohesive. There is no parapet and the octagonal corner-turrets terminate in pinnacles.

Rising from the top of the second stage is an octagonal broach-spire, the shoulders of which are visible behind the turrets; internally there would have been squinch-arches across the four corners of the tower. The spire is of four stages, separated by narrow bands of decoration (*cf.* Salisbury Cathedral), but it also has graduated lucarnes in the first three stages, as at

79 Fabris, c. 1735. Painting no. 1: north view of the Abbey, showing a version of Hawksmoor's scheme 4 for completing the western and crossing towers. WA Lib. Coll.

Lichfield Cathedral, which undoubtedly provided the principal source of inspiration for the design. For further discussion of the spire, see p. 66 and Figure 87.

An initial reaction might be that Fabris executed the first two paintings sometime before 1739, and the third painting in *c*. 1739–40, after the houses alongside the nave had been demolished. For several reasons, that cannot, however, be the case. There can be little doubt that the paintings were a set of three, or perhaps more, prepared to show alternative schemes for the completion of the Abbey. There is no record as to who commissioned the paintings, but it could well have been Hawksmoor himself. The buildings obscuring the lower parts of the nave and ambulatory were still standing, and other sources confirm that Fabris, in his first painting, depicted them both accurately and in their entirety. That establishes a date before 1739, when demolition of the houses began. In the second and third views he shows, respectively, the aesthetic effect of removing some, and all, of these structures. We know that a proposal to demolish the encumbrances around the Abbey was topical, and Wren had already advocated it at the beginning of the eighteenth century. Fabris's paintings appear to comprise a faithful record of the extant architectural detailing of the Abbey, and the omission of the small medieval doorway in the north aisle of the nave, from the third painting, is striking, but readily explicable. Until 1739 the doorway was obscured from view, being inside the building that abutted the nave, and thus the artist would not have known of its existence.[117] This provides another indication that all three paintings antedated the demolition of the houses. Had they been later, this door would surely have been included.

Thus, Fabris's views are intrinsically related to several of Hawksmoor's alternative schemes for completing both the western towers and the lantern tower. Moreover, it is clear that the third painting depicts Hawksmoor's final proposal, being the one which was chosen and, in large measure, brought to fruition. The raising of the north-west tower was commenced in the spring of 1735.[118] In January 1736/7 Hawksmoor was still hopeful that the lantern tower would be finished, but in the following month he reported that 'the House of Commons have suspended our fund for

80 *Fabris, c. 1735. Painting no. 1: detail of the proposed lantern tower from Figure 79, showing a variant of Hawksmoor's scheme 4, version (iii) (cf. Fig. 54). WA Lib. Coll.*

repairing the Abby'.[119] Nevertheless, funding was reinstated and work on the north-west tower was in progress when Hawksmoor died in March, and by 1738 it had been completed by his successor, John James. The latter then proceeded with the construction of the south-west tower, which was finished in 1745. The last of many annual grants had been voted by Parliament in the previous year and, a petition for further funding in December referred again to the desirability of building a spire above the crossing.[120] But, despite its express undertaking to 'complete' Westminster Abbey, no further funds were forthcoming from Parliament. Indeed, the Dean and Chapter had to beg for the final tranche of money in 1743, to avoid halting the building programme on the west front, when it was so close to completion. The House of Commons had been supporting the 'repairing and completing' of Westminster

81 *Fabris, c. 1735. Painting no. 2: north-west view of the Abbey, showing another version of Hawksmoor's scheme 4 for completing the western and crossing towers. WA Lib. Coll.*

Abbey since 1699, and about £149,000 had been expended on the work.[121] No further grants from the public purse would be made, and that spelled doom for the lantern tower proposal.

Fabris's paintings must precede all of the foregoing. It would have been pointless to commission a set of fine paintings, presenting a selection of alternative proposals by the architect, *after* a final decision had been made and construction work had commenced. Consequently, the paintings can hardly be later than 1735, and since we know that Hawksmoor was paid for his design for a spire over the crossing in May 1732, that fixes a *terminus post quem* for Fabris's commission. His inclusion of the tower of St Margaret's Church in its present form in paintings nos 1 and 2 provides another date indicator.[122] The church tower was restored and heightened by John James in 1734–35 but, as with the Abbey's towers, the scheme need not have been implemented

82 (left) Fabris, c. 1735. Painting no. 2: detail of the lantern tower from Figure 81, showing a variant of Hawksmoor's scheme 4, version (iii). WA Lib. Coll.

83 (below) Fabris, c. 1735. Painting no. 3: north view of the Abbey, showing Hawksmoor's final scheme for completing all the towers. © The Courtauld Institute of Art, London

The North West Prospect of Westminster Abby with the Spire as design'd by S.ʳ Christopher Wren.

84 *James and
Fourdrinier, 1737.
Engraving by Fourdrinier
of the north-west view
of the Abbey, from a
drawing by John James,
showing Hawksmoor's
western towers which were
then being completed. The
crossing tower and spire
are indicated in their
intended form. Although
the design is attributed
to Wren, this version
represents an amalgam
of four architects' work.
Wren Society 1934*

when Fabris painted his views. I therefore
conclude that the Fabris paintings should be
dated within the bracket 1732–35.

Hawksmoor's missing drawings of 1732 for
the upper stage of the lantern tower and spire
may yet come to light, as may Fabris's third
painting, which probably remains somewhere
in England. But his two other paintings – both
depicting rejected schemes – would have had
no particular significance any more, and it
may be deduced that he took at least one
of them back to Italy with him. The north
prospect (no. 1) appeared on the market in
Rome in 1826, when it was purchased and
brought back to England.[123] Far from being

'fantasy paintings', as they have often been
dismissed, Fabris's works constitute a crucial
component of the historical and architectural
record of Westminster Abbey in the eighteenth
century, and they are no less important than
Hawksmoor's drawings or his models. They all
go hand-in-hand.

It is not hard to see why the third Hawksmoor-
Fabris scheme was chosen, because it so
eloquently provided the correct visual balance
between the crossing and the west end. By
keeping the height of the western towers in
check, and resisting the temptation to add
spires to them, while at the same time imbuing
the crossing with a slim but soaring spire, the

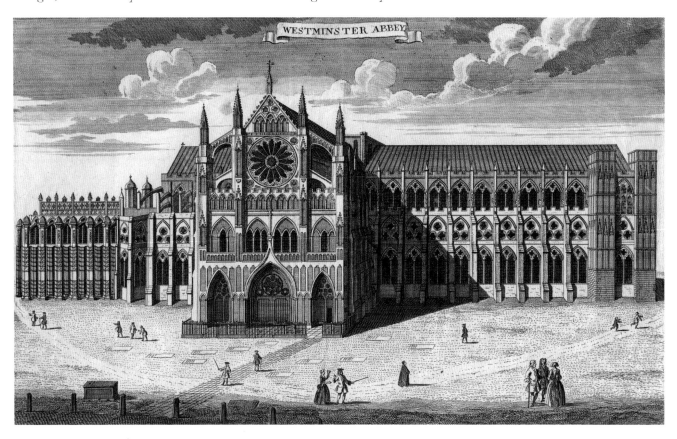

WESTMINSTER ABBEY

architect externally directed the beholder's focus on what is internally the most important part of the church. As Giles Worsley observed, the drawings show 'Hawksmoor grappling with the complex structural problems of restoring a great, decaying Gothic church, and the even more complex aesthetic issues of adding sympathetically to such a venerable structure'.[124]

As we have seen, in 1737 there was still an express intention to complete the lantern tower and spire according to Hawksmoor's design, adapted from Wren's initial proposal. It was probably immediately following Hawksmoor's death that James drew the north-west view of the 'completed' Abbey church, and Fourdrinier engraved it. [84] The engraving was published in a large format for sale to the public.[125] Nevertheless, numerous illustrations confirm that Hawksmoor's lantern was taken no higher than the string-course that now forms a temporary parapet, and that its appearance remained unchanged until 1941. A northern prospect of the Abbey, dating from *c.* 1730, clearly shows the square lantern with small windows and octagonal corner-turrets without

caps.[126] [85] Another view by Samuel Scott, 1739, depicts the Abbey from the north-east, also with the lantern in its present form.[127] Many further views, dating from the mid-eighteenth century onwards, show Hawksmoor's 'basement', complete with its lancet windows, octagonal corner-turrets and the moulded string-course upon which the lantern stage was to be built.[128]

The Mysterious Woodperry House Painting

Notwithstanding the foregoing, there is one further piece of evidence which introduces an element of mystery. An oil painting on canvas incorporated in the chimneypiece of the hall at Woodperry House, Stanton St John (Oxon.), depicts Westminster Abbey from the north-west, with the two western towers in their present form, and the crossing tower capped by a spire.[129] [86] The view of the Abbey is closely similar to Fabris's painting no. 3, but the setting is more panoramic, and overall it is closer to his painting no. 2. St Margaret's Church is also included in the view.[130] The

85 Anonymous, c. 1730. Engraving of the Abbey from the north, showing the completed basement stage of Hawksmoor's lantern tower, before work began on raising the north-west tower. WA Lib., Langley Coll. I.1.(5)

86 Unattributed: Mar[…], 1748. Detail from an oil painting incorporated in the hall chimneypiece at Woodperry House, Oxfordshire. This shows Hawksmoor's final scheme for the three towers at Westminster Abbey, and bears some resemblance to Fabris's painting no. 3 (Fig. 83) and Fourdrinier's engraving of 1737 (Fig. 84), although the latter lacks the surrounding buildings and townscape features. Author

Woodperry House painting, which bears an incompletely deciphered signature, is dated 1748.[131] It has been argued that the painting was based on one of Fourdrinier's engravings of 1737 [84], and the artist's viewpoint was undoubtedly the same in both.[132] The painting, however, is more life-like than the engraving, which is very 'flat' and lacks a convincing three-dimensional quality,[133] and there are significant differences of detail too. I am unconvinced that Fourdrinier's engraving even provided the source for the spire. Additionally, the engraving does not include St Margaret's Church or any of the other multitude of buildings and townscape features that are present in the painting. Consequently, the artist cannot have taken Fourdrinier's engraving alone as his

model, but must either have painted the scene on the spot (adding the spire), or diligently copied another artist's work. The artistry is good, particularly in the depiction of fine detail, and the archaeological content is impressively accurate in many respects. Demonstrably, this is not a fantasy painting executed in Oxford.

No convincing explanation has been advanced for the addition of this very fine painting to the principal chimneypiece in an Oxfordshire country house in 1748.[134] That the house should have been adorned with a painting of Westminster could be interpreted as a testimony to the public interest that was shown in the eighteenth century for seeing the Abbey completed. Curiously, though, once the raising of the western towers had been

accomplished, contemporary writers tired of the subject and did not enthuse about them in the way that one might have expected. The Woodperry painting thus postdates the high-point of public interest.

Although the drawings for Hawksmoor's intended lantern and spire have been lost, comparison of the three artists' illustrations is instructive and provides a clear picture of what would have been built, had not events been overtaken by the coronation of George II. [87] James's drawing shows the architectural detailing more precisely than the others, and it is clear that Hawksmoor derived his inspiration from the western spires of Lichfield Cathedral. All eight faces are pierced by lucarnes, arranged in three tiers: the

motivation for doing this at Westminster was doubtless to reduce as much as possible the gross weight of the spire. However, as drawn by James, the openings are too large, with the result that there is very little masonry at the angles to support the superstructure.[135] Unless a complex internal support structure was envisaged, this spire would have been unstable. The faces of the spire were to be embellished with panels of blind arcading beneath each lucarne, and three narrow decorative bands (seemingly of diminutive arcading) marking the divisions between the main stages. The latter detail represents a simplified version of Dickinson's proposal of 1722. [38]

The two paintings, on the other hand, show a structurally more realistic body of masonry at

87 *Details of the lantern tower and spire as depicted by (left to right): A. Fabris, painting no. 3, c. 1735; B. James and Fourdrinier, 1737; C. Woodperry House painting, Mar[...], 1748. Extracted from Figures 83, 84 and 86, respectively.*

the angles of the spire, and the lantern stage is also shorter. Moreover, their representation of the octagonal corner-turrets is more accurate: James shows them as square in plan, and diagonally set. No parapet is represented in any of the pictures, the spirelets crowning the turrets differ slightly, and only Fabris and James include a small pyramidal finial midway along each cardinal face.

8

James Wyatt
and the Fire of 1803

A Chapter minute of 5 May 1775 refers to the large openings in the sides of the lantern, which had been temporarily blocked by Hawksmoor in 1727 (p. 55), ordering that 'the four spaces in the dome, now boarded, be filled with chiaro scuro painting on oil cloth, according to the drawings produced. And also the centre circle on top of the dome with the same'.[136] This implies that William Kent's scheme had fallen out of fashion and was superseded, assuming that his paintings had been installed in the first place (p. 55).[137]

While we might have veered towards the conclusion that the arcading seen in the lantern in 1784 was not Kent's work of 1727, but was the *trompe l'oeil* painting ordered in 1775, it cannot be so because the latter appears unmistakably in Thomas Malton's engraving of the south transept in 1793. Malton shows that the chiaroscuro paintings simulated Gothic rose windows and filled only the blocked arches: they did not depict arcading.[138] [**88**] *Trompe l'oeil* tracery patterns executed in chiaroscuro were very popular at this period, particularly for wallpaper. The installation of the new paintings was effected by Henry Keene (Surveyor, 1752–76), just before his death. Hence, either the order given in 1775 was not carried out for at least nine years, or we have to accommodate a further phase of decoration for which no other evidence is known. There is an undeniable problem with the chronology, and for the time being the conundrum remains.

88 Malton, 1793. Detail from an engraving of the crossing, seen from the south transept, showing Hawksmoor's ceiling and trompe l'oeil painting of a rose window in the blocked arch on the north side of the lantern. WA Lib., Langley Coll. II.1.(22)

89 The central portion of Wyatt's vaulted plaster ceiling in the lantern. Photographed in 1937. WA Lib., RPHG neg. 1742

90 Neale, 1819. Engraving showing a section through the crossing and lantern tower, looking south. Neale and Brayley 1823

The Lantern Burns, July 1803

Keene was succeeded by James Wyatt (Surveyor, 1776–1813). He had evidently instructed roof repairs to be carried out on the lantern, where, on 9 July 1803, a fire occurred, caused by an

unattended workmen's brazier. Hawksmoor's roof and plaster vault were lost. The boarding in the lateral openings and the painted oil-cloth, 'placed here with execrable taste thirty years before', apparently held out against the fire, preventing it from spreading into the high roofs.[139] The architect-antiquary John Carter witnessed the conflagration, describing the event at great length and in melodramatic terms in the *Gentleman's Magazine*.[140]

> 'It was three o'clock this afternoon … on looking towards the Abbey Church I beheld the summit of the lantern, or great tower in the centre of the building, one entire blaze of fire. … I passed in by Poets' Corner, amidst rushing crowds, and armed volunteers. … Burning timbers of the roof, and groins (wood) tumbling down in dreadful crash; wide-spreading flames, clouds of smoke, rivers of water … by five o'clock the roof of the lantern and the greater part of the groins connected with them, had fallen on the pavement, putting an end to the horrid ravage …'

Carter recounts that a few days before the fire he had been on the roof of the Abbey (measuring and drawing), and 'I warned those present of the danger likely to ensue from the manner in which a portable furnace was left without any attendant, instancing the late fires at Boston church, Lincolnshire, Norwich Cathedral, Covent Garden church, etc.'

Wyatt's Reconstruction

The quire was out of use for nearly two years while Wyatt constructed a new roof over the lantern and another ornate, Gothic vaulted ceiling. Wyatt's vault was again of timber and plaster construction, embellished with numerous bosses in an admixture of styles (thirteenth century and Tudor).[141] [89] The plasterwork was by the notable stuccador Francis Bernasconi, who also created the reredos and high altar in 1823 (later destroyed). This time, the vault was not provided with an *oculus*. The lateral arches opening into the roof voids were infilled with plain brickwork, plastered on the inner face, and a central doorway was provided in each side. These features appear in several drawn sections through the crossing,[142] and also in early nineteenth-century views of the interior.[143] [90, 91, 92] Evidence of the fire is still discernible in the form of patches of blackening around the edges of the arches (as viewed from within the roof voids) where smoke penetrated between them and the inserted boarding.[144] [93] Wyatt's doors in the lantern were probably of timber,

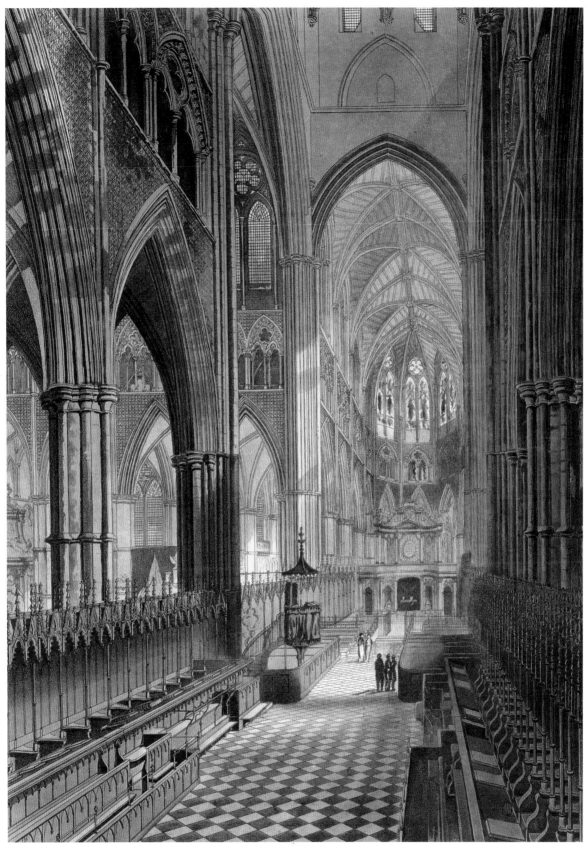

91 *Ackermann, 1812. The quire and crossing, looking east, showing the chequered marble floor of 1677 and the interior of the lantern. Ackermann 1812*

the present iron ones more likely being Scott's work.

A new low-pitched roof was constructed over the lantern which, most unusually, was covered with large slabs of Penrhyn slate, bedded in cement on boarding supported by timber trusses. [94] It is not recorded why Wyatt chose this unconventional method of roofing, but it may have been on account of the very exposed location, and the justifiable fear that lead sheeting could be lifted in a gale.[145] The roof and vault structures are recorded in published section drawings. [90] It also seems likely that Wyatt adapted the string-course around the top of the tower to form the unconventional parapet that we have today. Repairs were completed in 1805, and one of the workmen inscribed his name: 'D. HOUSDON 1805'.[146]

93 *Interior of the roof of the south transept, showing the large aperture in Hawksmoor's lantern, blocked with brickwork by Wyatt. Patches of smoke blackening on the edge of the arch resulted from the fire in 1803. Author*

94 *Roof of the lantern, from the south-east, in the 1870s. This shows Wyatt's slate slabs and two men working in the gutter. WA Lib., Langley Coll. I.3.(24)*

9

Sir George Gilbert Scott and 'some ameliorations in the Lantern'

Sir George Gilbert Scott (Surveyor, 1849–78) characteristically took an interest in the archaeological problem of the crossing tower: 'It is a question on which much difference of opinion exists, whether a central tower was ever contemplated'.[147] Uncharacteristically, though, he did not explore the subject in depth or reach a firm conclusion, musing, 'I cannot, however, think that the comparatively slender piers ... could have been intended to carry, at the most, more than a very light structure'. That was penned in 1859–60, before Scott became involved in the construction of new towers, and the wholesale restoration of medieval ones.[148] His *penchant* for designing soaring Gothic towers and spires was about to develop.

In the 1850s Scott was engaged on numerous restoration projects around the Abbey, and the slate roof of the lantern was repaired in 1856.[149] In the early 1860s he embarked on a major and expensive enhancement of the quire and sanctuary. It therefore occasions no surprise that he saw fit to tinker with the interior of the lantern, in an attempt to achieve a more purist Gothic feeling: he tersely described this work as making 'some ameliorations in the lantern'.[150] In 1859 the plain windows and high-level doorways were all cut out and embellished with new arch mouldings, flanking Purbeck marble shafts, hood-mouldings and label-stops.[151] The mouldings are in Box Hill Ground (Bath) stone. [95, 96] Painted inscriptions were added above the wall-arches, and the windows were filled with angels in stained glass by Clayton and

Bell. These were given by Lord John Thynne, Sub-Dean, in 1860.[152]

In 1866 Scott mentioned the fireproof iron doors to the openings, which he himself had probably installed in 1860.[153] [97] He also noted that the roof of the lantern was covered with slate slabs laid in cement on timber, an arrangement which is recorded in a photograph of the 1870s. [94] By this time, Scott was turning his attention to roof repairs, and doubtless had views on what should be done with the lantern. Unfortunately, they are not recorded, but it is highly likely that he would have given consideration either to the construction of a full-blown lantern tower or, at the very least, to 'finishing' the existing structure in what he considered to be an appropriate manner. The stumpy, featureless termination of the lantern would certainly not have satisfied Scott. Wherever he worked on Gothic buildings, he restored – or created anew – gables, parapets, crenellations, turrets and spirelets, all intensively decorated. We need look no further than the chapter house to witness Scott's appetite for Gothic embellishment.[154]

The chapter house was a huge and exhausting project for Scott (1866–72), and other urgent works on the Abbey (including roofs and the north portal) consumed the modest funds available for the fabric. Add to this, the fact that in 1869 the Ecclesiastical Commissioners sequestered almost all of the Abbey's ancient endowments, and that

95 *Interior of the west side of the lantern, showing Hawksmoor's windows and the large arch which was blocked by Wyatt in 1803. The windows and doorway were embellished with mouldings and Purbeck marble angle-shafts by Scott in 1860, and the stained glass is a mixture of Victorian fragments salvaged and reset in 1957. Author*

Scott suffered a breakdown in 1870, and it is clear that the opportunity for completing the lantern tower simply did not arise. But I am in no doubt that, given more favourable circumstances, Scott would have adorned the roofscape of Westminster Abbey with a grand Gothic centrepiece. Instead, one of his successors removed the slate slabs and laid a conventional lead roof on the lantern.[155] Scott does not mention the lantern in his autobiography, but the straightened

circumstances under which he operated are confirmed by his rueful remarks: 'My own works at the Abbey have not been extensive. ... I have planned a great sepulchral cloister on the south side ... but I see no prospect of its being carried into execution'.[156] Scott died in office in 1878, and his successor, J.L. Pearson (Surveyor, 1879–97), devoted much of his considerable energy to completing the drastic remodelling of the north transept.

96 *Detail of the doorway in the east side of the lantern, with Scott's added shafts and mouldings. Author*

97 Scott's iron door in the east side of the crossing, seen from the roof space over the presbytery. The smoke blackening on the brickwork above the door is the result of the fire in 1941. Author

10

The Early Twentieth Century,
World War II, and the Aftermath

J.T. Micklethwaite was appointed Surveyor of the Fabric in 1898, and in his second report to the Dean and Chapter he observed: 'The widening of Parliament Street has opened out a view of the north side of the church which has not existed before. And this has caused some newspapers to revive the old proposal to add a central tower and spire. As the suggestion is plausible, and one not unlikely to be popular, I take this opportunity to express my opinion that it is one which should not be entertained'.[157] His objection was based on the belief that the measures required to strengthen the crossing piers would be visually unacceptable. He conceded that the present tower 'has an unfinished look' and that it 'might be greatly improved without adding much to its weight, and that it would be well to do this'. Micklethwaite concluded: 'Little more than a good parapet and pinnacles is wanted to make it quite sightly'.

Nevertheless, a surge of nationalistic pride in the closing years of the nineteenth century, and the opening decade of the twentieth, sparked a desire, on the part of both Church and State, to create a new building at Westminster in which memorials to 'the great and the good' could be housed. The Abbey was full to overflowing with memorials, and something needed to be done to provide additional space. Various schemes were adumbrated by leading architects of the day.[158] One of these involved erecting a new building to the south-east of the chapter house, incorporating in it an enormous tower that would dwarf both Westminster Abbey and the nearby Victoria Tower in the Palace of Westminster. [98] The architects were J.P. Seddon and E.B. Lamb, and they published a scheme in 1904 for their 'Imperial Monumental Halls and Tower'.[159] An integral part of the scheme involved increasing the 'presence' of the Abbey by raising a large but unimaginative tower over the crossing. [99] The central towers at Canterbury and Wells may perhaps have provided their inspiration, but how they proposed to support this structure on the deformed crossing piers is not recorded.[160] The grandiose concept of building a national mausoleum soon afterwards faded away, like the potency of the British Empire, and none of the potential schemes was pursued to the design stage.

Fire-Bombed, May 1941

During the Second World War, the Abbey was hit by a number of incendiary bombs, and one of those fell on the roof of the lantern on the night of 10/11 May 1941. Had the roof still been covered with Wyatt's slate slabs, it may have been possible to deal with the offending device before the timbers of the roof ignited. That was not to be, and for the second time in 138 years the lantern tower became an inferno. Just as in 1803, the entire roof structure, together with the timber and plaster vault, were consumed *in situ* until they crashed down onto the marble pavement of the quire

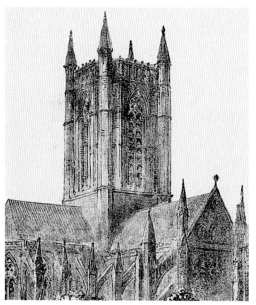

98 (above) Gaye, 1904. 'Design for the Imperial Monumental Halls and Tower, Westminster'. This scheme by Seddon and Lamb envisaged the erection of a dominant tower with a corona beside Westminster Abbey, and at the same time raising the height of the crossing tower considerably. View from the north-east. © RIBA Drawings Coll., Victoria and Albert Museum

99 Seddon and Lamb, 1904. Detail of Westminster Abbey with its proposed new crossing tower. View from the north-east. WA Lib. Coll.

below, where fire-fighters extinguished the burning débris. [**100**, **101**] The continuous rain of molten lead from the roof, onto the floor and quire stalls, was reported by eye-witnesses to be a spectacular element of the drama. The lantern roof, burning on the floor of the quire, was subsequently recorded in a tiny quarry in one of the stained glass windows installed in the chapter house in 1951.[161] [**102**]

Not only was Wyatt's timber and plaster vault destroyed, but so too were four of the Victorian stained glass windows in the lantern. The other four were badly damaged. However, because the tower acted as a chimney, the venturi effect caused the fire to burn upwards and, just as in 1803, the walls sustained very little damage. Nevertheless, it was reported that 'several tons of masonry from the injured lantern fell …'[162] Blackening of the brickwork around the iron doors, particularly on the east, shows how smoke, but not fire, penetrated the roof voids.

[**97**] The tower was quickly capped with a new roof of pyramidal form, comprising pre-cast concrete slabs supported on a steel framework. [**103**] The exterior was initially waterproofed with asphalt, rather than lead, and a concrete cap, cast *in situ*, was provided at the apex.

The structure was designed by B.L. Hurst and Peirce, civil engineers, and erected under the supervision of Sir Charles Peers (Surveyor, 1935–51).[163] [**104**, **105**] After the war, the manufacturers of 'Bison' concrete products, who had supplied the materials, published a photograph of the lantern roof in their trade brochure.[164]

Apart from clearing the débris and securing the damaged windows with clear glass, nothing else was apparently done to the lantern for the next fifteen years. However, while the scaffolding was in place in 1941, plumb-lines were set up against the crossing piers and three sets of measurements were taken for each. These recorded the verticality and bowing of each pier, at ten-foot intervals, on both its cardinal faces and on the diagonal (*i.e.* facing towards the centre of the crossing).[165] These measurements indicated that three of the piers had moved only very slightly outwards at the top – away from the centre of the crossing – but that on the north-west was more seriously

100 (above) The burnt-out lantern, 11 May 1941, showing the remnants of Wyatt's plaster vault. The painted inscription band around the crossing arch was added by Scott and obliterated by Dykes Bower in 1957. WA Lib. Coll.

101 (left) The remains of Wyatt's lantern roof and vault on the floor of the crossing, on the morning after the fire, 11 May 1941. The Dean, Paul de Labilliere, surveys the damage. WA Lib. Coll.

out-of-plumb (2¾ ins; 7 cm). All the piers are bowed fairly evenly throughout their height, the range being 2¼–3¾ ins (5.8–9.5 cm), with the exception of the north-west pier which is bowed by 5 ins (12.7 cm).

102 The timbers of Wyatt's lantern burning on the floor of the crossing in 1941, depicted in a quarry in the south-west window of the chapter house, by Joan Howson, 1951. View looking east towards the sanctuary. Author

103 The present lantern roof of concrete and steel, constructed after the fire in 1941. The lead covering was added later. Viewed from the south-east. WA Lib. Coll.

The temporary installation of clear glazing in the lantern increased the natural light-level in the upper part of the crossing, causing a heavy shadow to be cast by Hawksmoor's boldly projecting string-course; this seriously intruded upon the eye when looking eastwards along the nave, and broke up the visual continuity of the high vaults.[166]

Patching up the Lantern

It fell to Stephen Dykes Bower (Surveyor, 1951–73) to carry out reparations for the war damage, which was a tediously slow and bureaucratic process: many parts of the Abbey needed attention, some more urgently than others. Consequently, it was not until 1956–57 that, using funds obtained from the War Damage Commission, he was able to reinstate a ceiling over the lantern, to hide the hastily constructed concrete and steel roof of 1941. Dykes Bower also undertook minor repairs to the masonry and plasterwork, made good the damage to the chequered marble pavement of the quire,[167] and reglazed the lantern windows, alleviating the undesirable shadow-effect caused by the introduction of clear glass.[168] The glazing was carried out by Goddard and Gibbs, who salvaged some of the damaged glass and made up the existing 'salad' windows out of the fragments, mixing in also some Victorian glass recovered from the nave.[169] [**106**] Scott's painted inscriptions on the walls, although they survived the war, were unfashionable and were obliterated, while gold leaf was liberally applied to mouldings and head-stops. [**107**]

The destroyed ceiling was superseded by the present soffit by Dykes Bower in 1957. Funds were in short supply, and there was no possibility of reconstructing a vault or commissioning carved work. The simplest expedient was to erect an entirely flat timber ceiling, without mouldings, and to paint it. Accordingly, the new soffit was made of one-inch thick mahogany boards attached to timber joists supported by a framework of steel beams.[170] [**108**] Dykes Bower commonly sketched out rough proposals for his commissions, and then passed them to an assistant to work up. In this instance, the design for painting the lantern ceiling was duly worked upon by Hugh Mathew of Great Dunmow.[171] The drawings for the design layout, individual motifs and painting details are preserved.[172]

It is not difficult to trace sources for much

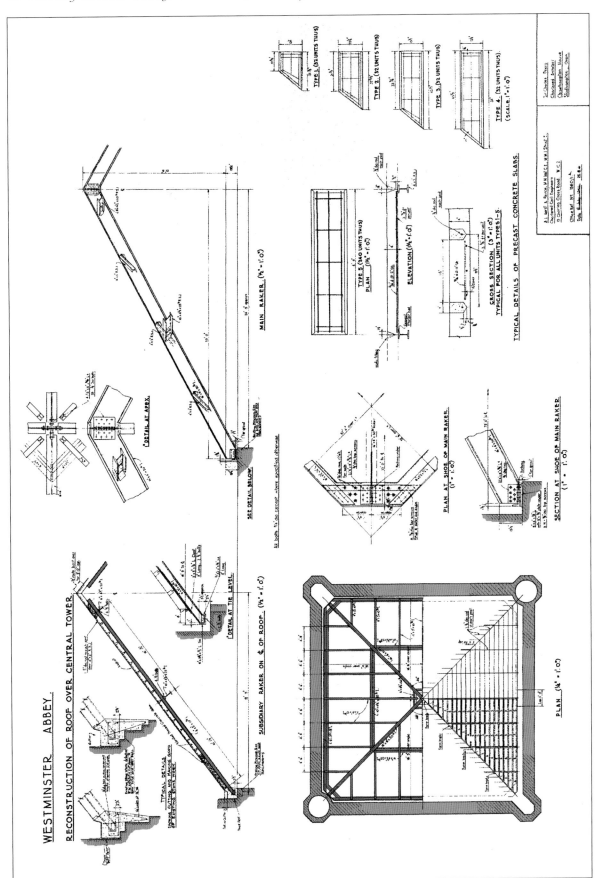

104 Hurst and Peirce, 1941. Engineers' design drawing for the concrete and steel roof installed over the crossing. WA Lib. Coll.

the Abbey, including in the Litlyngton Missal, which was perhaps the source of inspiration in this instance.[173] Other details are recognizably derived from Victorian floor tiles and medieval ornament in the Abbey. The design is overtly Puginesque. The colours are copied from the Pugin-Minton range of floor tiles, designed initially for the Palace of Westminster.[174] [**109**] Although highly decorative, the modern ceiling lacks the three-dimensional quality of Wyatt's vault, which was more successful in articulating what is otherwise a square hole in the roof of the Abbey, surmounted by a box. Dykes Bower simply put a flat lid on the box, making it possibly the seventh ceiling in recorded history to adorn Henry III's unfinished lantern.

Following the completion of war-damage repairs, Dykes Bower turned his attention to cleaning and decorating the interior of the Abbey, and to reconstructing the high roofs. The medieval timbers of the latter were showing signs of decay and, instead of carrying out sympathetic carpentry repairs, Dykes Bower embarked on a campaign of wholesale replacement, which involved the introduction of much concrete and steel as well as new timber. In a hugely expensive and publicly controversial campaign, he destroyed more of the historic fabric of Westminster Abbey in a

of the detailing. The basic geometry is simple, comprising a square with semicircles abutting its sides, a saltire in the middle and a rectangular border around the outside. The square-and-semicircles is a motif found in many places in

few years around 1970 than the Luftwaffe had managed in 1939–45.

Dykes Bower and the Crossing Tower: An Unfulfilled Desire?

The austerity of the post-war years militated against any ideas being put forward to make serious additions to the Abbey, but I suspect that Dykes Bower privately regarded his pleasing but simple ceiling in the lantern as no more than a medium-term measure, pending the day when a crossing tower could at last be built. He was an ardent admirer of the Abbey's western towers at a time when Hawksmoor's designs were not highly regarded by the architectural profession at large. I have little doubt that Dykes Bower would have wished, if possible, to complete the lantern according to Hawksmoor's design, and he might also have sketched out his own ideas for a lantern at the Abbey, even though he must have known that it would not fall to him to build it. By the early 1970s he did not, in any case, enjoy unbridled

popularity at Westminster, after the public opprobrium that he brought upon the Dean and Chapter over the roof *débâcle*. However, he clearly had an innate desire to construct a lantern tower, somewhere.

We have only to turn to St Edmundsbury Cathedral to appreciate how Dykes Bower's creative mind worked when he was given free-rein. Like Scott, he had grand visions and an obsession with Gothic detail. He was possessed with the desire to build a crossing tower in full-blown medieval Gothic style at Bury, and persuaded the Provost and Council that they should have one. In 1960–70, Dykes Bower undertook the reconstruction and enlargement of the eastern arm of the cathedral, at the same time adding a crossing, transepts and cloister. The walls of the crossing were taken up to roof-ridge level, and then a temporary cap placed over the whole, pending the day when funding could be found to add the lantern tower. Thus, in 1970 the extent of the nascent structure at Bury precisely corresponded to that which had been achieved at Westminster, first in *c.* 1260,

108 The crossing and lantern today, viewed from the floor. East is to the right. WA Lib. Coll.

109 *Painted timber ceiling of the lantern by Dykes Bower, 1957. WA Lib. coll.*

and again in 1727. At the time of Dykes Bower's death in 1994, funding for the lantern tower had still not been secured, and so he bequeathed the cathedral £2 million as a pump-primer. Eventually, the Cathedral Council adopted the construction of the lantern tower as its Millennium project. Funds were raised, and it was duly completed in 2005.

From Westminster's viewpoint, there is an additional irony to this story, which is not widely known. Dykes Bower's bequest to St Edmundsbury was conditional upon the cathedral authorities building a lantern tower: if they declined to do so, the £2 million was to be reallocated to Westminster Abbey.

The only work undertaken on the lantern since Dykes Bower's surveyorship has been the introduction of high-level electric light fittings mounted on steel frames in 1988.[175]

11

New Surveys of the Crossing and Lantern, 2009–10

The lantern tower has not hitherto been the subject of a detailed structural, architectural or archaeological study, and until now no accurate drawings of it have existed. As part of a long-term project to compile a three-dimensional, digitally-based record of the entire structure of Westminster Abbey, the crossing and adjacent areas of the church were fully surveyed in 2009–10.[176] From the plans, elevations and section drawings thereby produced, it is now possible to understand more fully the construction of the tower, and to measure precisely the amount of movement that has taken place in each of the main piers. The measurements generally confirm the observations made in 1941 (p. 83), that the north-west pier is more out-of-plumb than the others, and that the bowing of the shafts (measured on the diagonals) is 12.5 cm on the north-west pier, but is less than 10 cm on the other three.[177] Demonstrably, there has been no significant change in the last sixty years, and since there is no sign of failure in Hawksmoor's masonry repairs of the 1720s, it may be concluded that the crossing has been structurally stable for three hundred years, or more.

Wren attributed the bowing of the crossing piers to the failure of Henry III's masons to build the lantern tower immediately, and hence to load the structure with sufficient dead-weight to prevent the lateral thrusts exerted by the arcades from distorting them (p. 31). Some commentators, including Sir Gilbert Scott, have wondered whether the tall, slender piers

of the crossing would ever have been capable of supporting a substantial tower and spire. Did Henry of Reyns over-reach himself and attempt to erect a structure that was inherently unstable and would have failed anyway, even if it had been completed?

Despite misgivings by some architectural historians, one has only to look at the great thirteenth-century churches of France to appreciate that lofty crossings could and often did support masonry towers, lanterns and spires of breathtaking height and complexity. Monumental towers had been built in western Europe for upwards of three centuries, and all without the benefit of engineering calculations. The approach was purely empirical, and a large body of practical knowledge had been amassed. Thus when designing the crossing at Westminster, Henry of Reyns would have been able to draw on centuries of experience of French masons. With the benefit of modern structural engineering knowledge, it is now possible to analyze the existing fabric and to determine how much load the crossing piers (in their original unbowed state) could have borne without failing. These calculations have recently been made, with surprising results.[178]

One of the areas of critical concern from a structural engineering point of view is the nature of the foundations upon which Henry III's crossing was built: the strength of the substructure is of no less importance than that of the superstructure. Remarkably, very little information is currently available on the subject of the Abbey's foundations, but in September 2009, *Time Team* conducted an archaeological excavation outside the nave, to the west of the north transept, and this revealed that the mid-thirteenth-century transept wall and its buttresses stand on a massive, stepped raft built of mortared masonry. The full depth was not ascertained during the 2009 investigation, but from observations made in the nineteenth century it is believed to be in the region of 3.0 m.[179] It seems likely that the buttressed outer walls and the arcades of the transept and nave aisles stand on huge rafts of solid masonry, and do not have separate strip-foundations. This was expressly confirmed in the case of the eastern aisle of the south transept by an excavation which was carried out in 1938 to investigate a grave in the centre of the southernmost bay. The grave, which was 1.12 m deep, had been cut entirely into solid foundation masonry.[180] Various boreholes and deep excavations in the near vicinity of the Abbey have yielded data on the depth and nature of the natural deposits of gravel and clay that form the bedrock of the site. These data provide further evidence to assist the structural calculations, which have confirmed that the foundations are strong enough to support an additional 1,200 tons of masonry at the crossing.[181]

Next, the structure of the crossing piers themselves was investigated. For one-third of their height, these are freestanding columns cut from massive blocks of Purbeck marble, a material which can withstand enormous weight under compression, without the stone crushing. For the remaining two-thirds of their height the crossing piers are integrated with the masonry of the triforium and clearstorey. [8] Consequently, the effective cross-section of masonry comprises a mixture of Purbeck marble and Caen stone: the latter has less ability to resist crushing under compression than the former. Since the structural strength of the crossing is only as good as its weakest

component, that had to be identified and engineering calculations applied on it. The weakest point lies at the interface between the freestanding column and the beginning of the composite masonry of the triforium, *i.e.* immediately above the level of the main arcade capitals. Again, engineering calculations demonstrated that the tower, as originally built, could have taken an additional 1,200 tons of loading, over and above the existing masonry. Consequently, prior to the bowing of the crossing piers, there would have been sufficient structural support for Henry III to have crowned the Abbey with a great lantern tower. By the same token, there would have been no problem with supporting the tower and spire that Wren envisaged.

As part of a general survey of the structure and condition of the floors throughout the Abbey, ground-penetrating radar (GPR) is being used to map the sub-surface topography.[182] The results obtained in the crossing and transepts have proved most interesting, revealing the complex honeycomb of the underfloor vaults and shafts constructed to receive post-medieval burials. While both transepts have been used intensively for burial, it is surprising to find that the crossing is apparently devoid of tombs, with a single exception at the centre. The radar scans indicate that the chambers are between 1.0 m and 1.5 m in depth, and have not therefore interfered with the foundation structure to any significant degree. Unfortunately, it has not been possible to detect the lateral extent of the foundations of Henry III's work within the abbey church. In particular we cannot be sure, without archaeological investigation beneath the floor, whether the four crossing piers rise from individual foundations, or are linked together by continuous strip-foundations. The arcades that adjoin the crossing on all sides almost certainly have continuous foundation rafts under their piers, and these may also encompass the crossing itself, although that remains to be demonstrated.

12

Summary
and Conclusions

There are few documentary references to the crossing tower at Westminster Abbey and, despite being of crucial importance in the English coronation ceremonial, the architectural history of this part of the abbey church has never been seriously studied. The evidence of the Bayeux Tapestry confirms that nine-hundred-and-fifty years ago, the crossing was crowned by a prominent tower and lantern, erected by Edward the Confessor. Then Henry III, two hundred years later, rebuilt much of the church and raised a lofty new crossing, but never completed the tower and lantern above roof level. However, consideration of the design aesthetics of the church as a whole, comparisons with contemporary French architecture, and a modest amount of archaeological evidence, all combine to suggest that the crossing was intended to support an octagonal lantern and a spire or *flèche*, all set within a quartet of octagonal corner-turrets. This feature would have been intended to dominate both the exterior of the church and the skyline of Westminster.

For about a century after Henry's death in 1272, the rebuilding programme stagnated, but sometime before the sixteenth century an octagonal stone lantern, supporting a timber-framed cupola was erected on the existing stump over the crossing. Arguably, this occurred around the end of the fourteenth century, when the Abbey's building programme was restarted. If this dating is correct, then the architect is likely to have been Henry Yeveley, the King's Master Mason. The lantern, which appears in a drawing of 1532, looks like a smaller, simpler version of the famous octagon at Ely, and may have been very similar to the lost lantern of Peterborough Cathedral.

The chance survival of three drawings dating from the first half of the sixteenth century not only records the existence of the later medieval lantern, but also its destruction by *c.* 1544, leaving a windowless, box-like enclosure over the crossing. Although acknowledged to be unsatisfactory, this situation obtained until the end of the seventeenth century, when the Dean and Chapter determined to improve the Abbey's somewhat run-down image, and Parliament voted substantial funds to 'repair and complete' the building.

A feature which has frequently given rise to comment, since the early sixteenth century, is the slight inward bowing of the four crossing piers. This was caused by the combined lateral thrusts exerted upon them by the main arcades and the triforium arches, and it is clear that deformation occurred very soon after construction (probably before the end of the thirteenth century). Centuries later, Sir Christopher Wren's assessment of the situation was most likely correct: had Henry III completed the construction of his crossing tower and lantern, the superincumbent weight of masonry would have countered the propensity of the piers to bow. Recent engineering calculations have confirmed that, notwithstanding its elegant and slender proportions, the crossing was fully capable of supporting a great lantern and spire.

The decision was made in 1697 to complete the three unfinished towers of Westminster Abbey, and Wren was charged with the task. At the opening of the eighteenth century we enter an era from which the first architectural drawings of the Abbey have survived, these being the products of Wren, his assistants and successors, most notably William Dickinson and Nicholas Hawksmoor. Also extant are the minutes of some meetings, a few letters, various bills, and other documents relating to a range of proposals for the erection of a tower and spire – or, alternatively, for a cupola – over the crossing. Additionally, scale models in timber and stone were made of the crossing, or parts of it, to illustrate architects' proposals in the early eighteenth century. Wren's magnificent oak model survives in the Abbey Collection, as do fragments of Hawksmoor's stone model. Finally, by the mid-seventeenth century, topographical artists and architectural draughtsmen were beginning to record the building in more detail than had been attempted hitherto, thus providing a valuable and continuing record of developments.

Welcome though all this additional evidence is, it does not add up to a comprehensive and easily read narrative in respect of the later history of the crossing tower: only a tiny proportion of the documentation that must once have existed has survived; half of the extant drawings are undated; some have been modified to show variant designs; and most relate to unexecuted schemes. Moreover, some of the works by topographical artists accurately reflect the appearance of the Abbey, while others show proposals; also, captions claiming that Wren was responsible for the schemes illustrated are not always accurate, and designs wholly or partly by his successors have been attributed to him. Nevertheless, Wren's comprehension of the need to complete the crossing in a worthy manner was soundly based and his inspiration was long-enduring. Add to this, the three remarkable paintings by Pietro Fabris, the true purpose of which has never before been explained – they have been dismissed as mere 'fantasies' – and it is small wonder that the architectural history of the lantern in the eighteenth century has remained obscure. However, research shows that it need not be.

Every architectural account of the works of Wren and Hawksmoor mentions the western towers at Westminster and notes the survival of a few related drawings, but the archaeological evidence for the crossing tower, preserved in the fabric itself, has neither been recorded nor considered capable of contributing to the overall picture. Yet it is critical. In short, the full gamut of historical and archaeological evidence, from the mid-thirteenth century to the mid-twentieth, can be assembled and arranged in a plausible sequence. It may be compared to a jigsaw puzzle with half the pieces missing: it is possible to make some secure connections, and arrange other fragments in such a way as to reveal the basics of the original design. Consequently, when the totality of the extant evidence has been laid out in an orderly fashion, an intelligible pattern begins to emerge, and more knowledge could be recovered through detailed archaeological study and recording of the fabric when the lantern is next scaffolded.

Both Wren and Hawksmoor appreciated that the focal point of coronation was all-important and that the central tower needed to dominate Westminster Abbey, not the western towers. Although the reasoning would have been different in the thirteenth century, the emphasis would certainly have been on the crossing, as was manifest in many great French churches. The western towers were always intended to be subordinate in the architectural hierarchy of the building, and it was doubtless that reasoning which led to the rejection of Hawksmoor's schemes which involved topping them with short spires. Until the secular buildings which were close to the Abbey were demolished in the eighteenth and nineteenth centuries, and Victoria Street was laid out (1851), the west end of the church did not constitute a prominent façade.

Two other aspects were of far greater importance, and had been so since the thirteenth century. First, there was the view of the Abbey from the king's lodgings in the Palace of Westminster to the east. It may have been no accident that the west door of his hall (known as the White or Lesser Hall) was aligned with the axis of the Abbey church (*cf.* Figure 4), and the symbolic importance of marking the crossing with a soaring tower or spire which would rise well above all the apses is self-evident.[183] The absence of such a feature gives the impression today that the Abbey has its back turned

*110 Amiens Cathedral.
The axial approach to
the south transept portal,
with the flèche rising
above the crossing and
dominating the skyline.
© The Courtauld
Institute of Art, London*

towards the Palace. The second important view was that seen when approaching the Abbey from the north. The great portal in the north transept was the royal entrance, and the processional route leading directly to it was aptly named King Street. While the transept gable has always been dignified with a series of large pinnacles, rising axially behind these and dominating the skyline above should have been the crossing lantern and spire. Such an arrangement still obtains in some of the great continental churches, such as Amiens Cathedral. [**110**]

Hence, it is readily apparent that the ungainly stump of tower we see today does not itself represent a *complete* structure of any date, but is manifestly only the beginning of a scheme that was prematurely halted. When we marry the extant physical evidence with the appropriate drawings by Hawksmoor, one of Fabris's paintings (no. 3), and the Woodperry chimneypiece, we can readily comprehend the full picture. In 1727, a square lantern tower with corner pinnacles and a tall, slender spire was under construction, but work had to be halted, the scaffolding removed and the crossing made seemly for the coronation of King George II in October of that year. Had it not been for the death of George I and the consequent coronation, the lantern tower would almost certainly have been finished according to the design depicted in the paintings, with the western towers following on subsequently. In the event, after the coronation, attention turned to the western towers, which were duly completed according to Hawksmoor's final scheme. Then in 1743, just when it was expected to resume work on the lantern, Parliament terminated its series of annual grants for 'repairing and completing' the Abbey. We can only assume that, as late as 1748, there was still an expectation that the lantern tower would be completed: otherwise there is no logical explanation for its depiction in the Woodperry painting.

Throughout the ensuing two-hundred-and-sixty years, the manifestly incomplete state of the lantern, and its unworthiness to cap the crossing of Westminster Abbey, has been a constant source of comment. The lantern has twice been burnt out – in 1803 and 1941 – and has been repaired and tinkered with by Wyatt, Scott and Dykes Bower. But it still remains just as unsatisfactory and 'temporary' looking, and continues to stand out as a very visible challenge for completion. Both Scott and Dykes Bower were admirers and builders of Gothic towers, but during their respective surveyorships at Westminster circumstances were not conducive to embarking on such a major construction project. Had the opportunity arisen, both would undoubtedly have relished the challenge of fulfilling Parliament's mandate in 1697 of 'completing' Westminster Abbey.

One fact, however, is not in doubt: for almost a thousand years Westminster Abbey has either had, or been intended to have, a lantern tower rising majestically above the crossing.

Appendix

Function and Variety in Early Crossing Towers and their Superstructures

by Richard Gem

The history of the central tower at Westminster Abbey is known in some detail, from the time of Edward the Confessor up until the last interventions in the twentieth century, and has been admirably analysed by Dr Warwick Rodwell. These developments at Westminster can be set into their architectural context in England and on the Continent, where a wide range of surviving structures provide contemporary parallels. However, what may not be so well appreciated is that there was once a much greater diversity of superstructures above central towers than is now represented by the extant examples. In particular, we have lost all spires earlier than the twelfth century, and with them a range of types of early origin. It may, therefore, be relevant to a consideration of the background of the central tower of Westminster Abbey to draw attention here to this greater diversity that once existed, as well as to place such structures in their religious context.[184]

Late Antiquity

In many typical early Christian churches the altar stood towards one end of the building within an area in front of the apse, while the apse itself provided seating for the presiding clergy. The apse and the area in front of it constituted the presbytery or sanctuary of the church (the sacrarium in Westminster terminology) and this area was enclosed by low chancel screens.

A trend towards the architectural enhancement of the bay containing the altar and presbytery led to the emergence of the axial lantern tower. Such towers are first recorded in France in the sixth century, as at Nantes Cathedral and the church of Saint-Anatolien at Clermont Ferrand, but no examples of these survive. However, the type is represented by the extant church of San Salvatore at Spoleto, in central Italy. This had a low tower with lantern windows admitting a flood of light into the presbytery area. At Spoleto the tower has a stone vault, but at Clermont there was a painted ceiling.

Also in sixth-century France can be traced the origin of elaborate timber superstructures over churches; these in contemporary sources were often called *machinae*, 'contrivances'. At the famous basilica of St Martin at Tours in the sixth century the tower over the east sanctuary was surmounted by such a superstructure. A later description of the church at Tours says that: 'the *machina* of the church shining in the sun seemed like a small mountain of gold'. We do not know the specific architectural form that such *machinae* took, but from passing references it is clear that they were elaborate openwork structures built in timber and clad in lead or copper, with decoration in gilding and tinning.

The Early Middle Ages

With the growing importance of the monastic order in the early Middle Ages, appropriate space had to be found in churches for the monks. The monks occupied a status between the ordained clergy and the laity, and accordingly were stationed in churches between the screened-off presbytery and the general congregational nave. Furthermore, since the singing of the office (at matins, vespers and the other day and night hours) took up more of the daily liturgical round than the celebration of the Eucharist itself, the area of the monks' choir attained increasing importance.

One architectural consequence of this development was that the monks' choir came to occupy the area under the lantern tower, while the presbytery and altar were accommodated in an extended arm of the building to the east of the tower. The tower in such an arrangement might be flanked by transept arms to the north and south – whence the modern term 'crossing tower'. Such an arrangement is shown already in the famous idealized plan of a monastery drawn for presentation to the abbot of Sankt Gallen (Switzerland) in the early ninth century.

Also in the early medieval period timber superstructures above churches (whether rising from a tower or from the main roof) became increasingly elaborate, and they frequently contained bells. In the third quarter of the eighth century at the royal abbey of Saint-Denis, near Paris, the king had erected over the basilica a 30-ft high *casubula* ('adornment'), enriched with gilding and silvering. A generation later, in 801, the international Anglo-Saxon scholar Alcuin sent to the archbishop of York a quantity of tin for the roof of the bell-cote of his cathedral. At the abbey of Saint-Wandrille in Normandy an early ninth-century abbot erected over the tower of his church: 'a pyramid, square in plan, 35 ft high, constructed of turned wood, covered with lead, tin and gilded copper, and he placed three bells in it'.

The most elaborate such tower super-structure known from the ninth century was at the abbey of Saint-Bertin in north-east France, where it replaced an earlier more modest turret. This doubled the height of the church and was constructed of timber in three stages, not including the bell-cote surmounted by an orb and cross. Each stage was circular in plan, and presumably set back above the one below it; while a central mast ran through the whole.

None of these elaborate ninth-century structures survives, but an eleventh-century illustration of the abbey of Saint-Riquier, also in north-east France, showed the contemporary church with elaborate staged superstructures rising above cylindrical towers at both the east and west ends of the building. [111]

The Later Middle Ages

A development seen in some later medieval churches was to move the monks' choir from the crossing into a greatly extended eastern arm that contained also the presbytery – as happened at Canterbury Cathedral in the early twelfth century. In such cases the tower over the crossing was left as a somewhat meaningless architectural statement, since it surmounted an empty space. But many churches did not follow this route, and the tower remained as an emphatic point over the liturgical area between the east end of the choir and the high altar. The contemporary biography of King Edward the Confessor states that in his rebuilding of Westminster Abbey the elaborate central tower was intended to rise above the crossing 'which was to surround the central choir of those singing to God'; while the dedications of the chapels on two levels in the transept arms to either side might be seen as joining the company of saints with the devotions of the choir. This arrangement was modified but certainly not abandoned in the rebuilding under Henry III.

During the later Middle Ages in England the crossing tower received ever greater arch-itectural elaboration and height as, for example, at St Albans Abbey and Norwich Cathedral in the eleventh and twelfth centuries, through to Durham and Canterbury cathedrals in the fifteenth and sixteenth centuries. Alongside such major towers built on a square plan, there appeared elsewhere in England polygonal towers rising over lesser churches; while the octagonal lantern at Westminster Abbey depicted in the Islip Roll itself shows such forms were not alien to major churches. (It may

111 *Saint-Riquier abbey. View from the south, showing the Carolingian staged lantern towers above the crossing and at the west end of the church. Hubert et al. 1970*

also be noted that on the Continent elaborate polygonal towers were commonplace on major Romanesque churches.) Generally speaking, later medieval English towers were either capped with simple roofs or were surmounted by lofty spires constructed in stone or lead-covered timber. The technological masterpiece in this genre, the spire of Salisbury Cathedral, has become an iconic image through the paintings of John Constable.

But the preponderance of the spire among surviving examples should not lead to the assumption that this was the only form of tower superstructure adopted by the builders of the later Middle Ages. In north-east France at the abbey of Corbie an illustration of the church before its destruction at the Revolution shows a three-staged openwork structure over the west tower that, while it may perpetuate an idea going back several centuries, was clearly built in the Gothic style. [27] Meanwhile in England the famous fourteenth-century Octagon of Ely Cathedral shows the adoption of an elaborate lead-clad timber structure over the crossing: this was immediately in response to the collapse of the previous crossing tower; but at the same time the designer may have been aware of the inheritance of an earlier and continuing tradition in which the structure over the crossing of a church could be innovative and structurally exciting.

A somewhat different situation is represented by the well-known fifteenth-century west tower of St Nicholas in Newcastle (now

the cathedral) and the crossing tower of the High Church of Edinburgh (St Giles), where a crown of four intersecting ogee arches rise to a central pinnacle, all built in stone. The origins of this arrangement are unknown, but conceivably lie in lost timber constructions.

Conclusions

Historical precedent shows that church towers and their superstructures originated and continued as outward architectural statements of the inward religious function of the buildings over which they rose, emphasizing the liturgical heart of the church and providing light above it.

Evidence from the sixth century onwards points to a wide variety of *forms* being employed in crossing towers and their surmounting superstructures. Equally there was a wide variety of *materials* deployed, including stone, timber and metals (lead, copper, tin, silver and gold), used for both practical and ornamental reasons.

The greatest era of experimentation may have lain in the period of late antiquity and the early Middle Ages, while in the later Middle Ages there may have been a tendency towards elaboration on the basis of more standardized forms. Nonetheless, precedents do occur for the adoption of more experimental forms at later dates and show that these were not considered by contemporaries as incompatible with the Gothic style.

Notes
and References

WA Lib. = Westminster Abbey Library
WAM = Westminster Abbey Muniments

1   The tower could be interpreted as having an octagonal upper stage, but certainty is impossible. The surviving crossing tower at Jumièges, Normandy – which is the closest analogue for Edward's abbey church – is square throughout its height, but its twin western towers have square bases and octagonal upper stages.

2   R.D.H. Gem, 'The Romanesque Rebuilding of Westminster Abbey', *Proceedings of the Battle Conference on Anglo-Norman Studies, III, 1980*, fig. 5 (Woodbridge, 1981). Dr Gem's reconstruction, which is reproduced here (Fig. 3), envisages a pyramidal roof to the crossing tower, not a domical cupola-like termination, and circular corner-turrets with conical roofs. The turrets could equally well have been square with pyramidal roofs.

3   J. Hubert, J, Porcher and W.F. Volbach, *Carolingian Art*, pl. 2 (London, 1970).

4   T. Tatton-Brown, 'The Building History of the Lady Chapels', in T. Tatton-Brown and R. Mortimer (eds.), *Westminster Abbey: The Lady Chapel of Henry VII*, 189–204 (Woodbridge, 2003); for the plan, see fig. 5.

5   The nationality of Henry of Reyns has been much debated, and current opinion favours English parentage, rather than French; however, this is by no means certain.

6   A.E. Henderson, *Westminster Abbey Then and Now* (SPCK, London, 1937).

7   C. Wilson, 'The Chapter House of Westminster Abbey: Harbinger of a New Dispensation in English Architecture?', in W. Rodwell and R. Mortimer (eds.), *Westminster Abbey Chapter House: The History, Art and Architecture of 'a chapter house beyond compare'*, 40–65 (Society of Antiquaries, London, 2010).

8   S. Murray, *Notre-Dame, Cathedral of Amiens*, pl. 7 (Cambridge, 1996).

9   The exact overall dimensions of the crossing piers above plinth level (excluding the attached shafts) are 13.3 m (north–south) by 13.5 m (east–west).

10 Close access for inspection is not possible without scaffolding, but most of the moulded masonry in the Henrician work, if not of Purbeck marble is of Caen Stone. Reigate stone was generally used for plain ashlar and rubble-work.

11 For a plan showing the relationship of the bell-tower to the Abbey church, see R. Thomas, R. Cowie and J. Sidell, *The Royal Palace, Abbey and Town of Westminster on Thorney Island*, fig. 45. Museum of London Archaeology Service, Mono. **22** (London, 2006).

12 Previously noted in W.R. Lethaby, *Westminster Abbey Re-Examined*, 62 (London, 1925).

13 I use the term 'nave' in an architectural sense throughout this study, to refer to the main vessel of the church, west of the crossing; liturgically, however, the three easternmost bays of the nave, as well as the crossing itself, were occupied by the quire at Westminster, as in many other great churches.

14 The survival of this masonry inside the attached stair-turrets is incompatible with the demolition of a putative square tower; on the other hand, it can be explained if there had been an octagonal tower with projecting or detached corner-turrets (p. 16).

15 Pipe Roll 2 Edward I, rot. 18d. Cited in H. Colvin (ed.), *The History of the King's Works*, **1**, 146, n. 7 (HMSO, London, 1963).

16 In plan, at eaves level the tower measured 13.3 m (east–west) by 13.45 m (north–south), overall.

17 J. Bony, *French Cathedrals*, pls 85 and 86 (London, 1951).

18 There has been a reluctance by previous writers to accept the existence of this lantern, although no cogent argument for dismissing the graphic evidence has been advanced. Thus, it has been described as 'a mere symbol rather than a representation': W.R. Lethaby, *Westminster Abbey and the King's Craftsmen*, 91 (London, 1906).

19   Tapisserie Plan: Musée Notre-Dame. I am grateful to Tim Tatton-Brown for supplying a copy of the drawing. See also A. Erlande-Brandenburg, *Notre-Dame de Paris* (Abradale Press, New York, 1999).

20   *Wren Soc.* **11** (1934), 19.

21   Bodleian Library: Gough Mss. Reproduced in *Wren Soc.* **11**, pl. 4.

22   W.H. St John Hope, *The Obituary Roll of John Islip, Abbot of Westminster, 1500–1532, with Notes on other English Obituary Rolls.* Vetusta Monumenta VII (Society of Antiquaries, London, 1906). For discussion of Islip's roll, see pp. 11–13; the letter is illustrated on pl. 24.

23   The Islip Roll was included in the Royal Academy's, *Exhibition of Flemish Art, 1300–1700*, in 1953–54: cat. no. 625. The drawings were previously attributed to Hans Holbein.

24   The plain pyramidal roof on the cupola may well represent a simplification by the artist, since it would have been impossible for him to incorporate a tall spire or *flèche* in this elaborated letter 'U'.

25   B. Willis, *A Survey of the Cathedrals*, **2**, engraving by J. Harris opp. 332 (London, 1742); J. Maddison, *Ely Cathedral: Design and Meaning*, 63–70, fig. 53 (Ely Cathedral Publications, 2000).

26   D. King, *The Cathedrall and Conventuall Churches of England and Wales, Orthographically Delineated*, fig. 23 (London, 1656); L. Reilly, *An Architectural History of Peterborough Cathedral*, 28, pl. 43 (Oxford, 1997).

27   For construction details of the Ely octagon, see C.A. Hewett, *English Cathedral and Monastic Carpentry*, 114–22 (Chichester, 1985).

28   A. Peigné-Delacourt, *Monasticon Galliarum*, **2**, pl. 76 (Paris, 1871).

29   H. Keepe, *Monumenta Westmonasteriensia*, 131 (London, 1683).

30   J. Dart, *History of St Peter's, Westminster*, **2**, 58 (London, 1723).

31   One or two bells could be tolled from a platform or gallery within the lantern, and that presents no great logistical problem. However, installing a peel of six for change-ringing is quite a different matter. The bells could not have been rung from the floor of the quire, both on account of the distance being too great, and the inconvenience it would cause to the conduct of services. Hence, a ringing chamber would have to be constructed inside the lantern, and that had to be separated from the belfry itself, on account of the noise factor.

32   For detailed drawings of the timberwork, see *The Builder* **93**, 3 Aug. 1907.

33   H.A. Cox and H.W. Brewer, *Old London Illustrated. London in the XVI Century*, fig. 10 (*The Builder*, 8th edn., London [1947]). Brewer's drawing appears to be dated 1894.

34   C. Wilson, in Rodwell and Mortimer 2010, *op. cit.*, 56, fig. 62. The drawing is in the Victoria and Albert Museum: E.128–1924.

35   Being without purlins or wind-braces, the thirteenth-century rafter-couples of the high roofs of the Abbey relied upon their being securely held in the vertical plane by large masses of masonry at both ends. Diagonal braces were later fitted, at

36   H. Colvin and S. Foister (eds.), *The Panorama of London, circa 1544, by Anthonis van den Wyngaerde.* London Topographical Soc., **151** (1996). The original drawings which make up the panorama are in the Bodleian Library, Oxford. They were previously published by London Topographical Society in their vols **1** (1881–82) and **77** (1941).

37   *E.g.* N. Whittock, *London, Westminster and Southwark as they appeared A.D. 1543*, fig. 1. (London, n.d., *c.* 1840).

38   G.E. Mitton, *Maps of Old London*, fig. 1 (London, 1908).

39   Another introduction is St Margaret's church, which was omitted from the original drawing; and the *campanile* is shown in a markedly different form.

40   Although the drawing may represent the situation obtaining in 1532, it is more likely to have been based on an earlier record that depicted the coronation in 1509. Hence, the possibility that the lantern had already been lost before 1532 must be acknowledged.

41   For the north elevation, see M. Roberts, *Dugdale and Hollar: History Illustrated*, 59 (University of Delaware Press, 2002). For the south elevation, see *Wren Soc.* **11**, pl. 1. Typically, Hollar omitted the cloister ranges entirely, 'completing' the architectural detail on the south elevation as though there had never been any abutments.

42   J.C. Keirincx's prospect of Westminster (1625) is a very elementary sketch and the detailing is possibly not reliable; it is reproduced in I. Watson, *Westminster and Pimlico Past: A Visual History*, fig. 1 (Historical Publications, London, 2002).

43   Watson 2002, *op. cit.*, fig. 1.

44   Bodleian Library, Gough Mss. Reproduced in *Wren Soc.* **11**, 115, pl. 4.

45   The positioning of these eight openings points to an octagonal or even circular gallery arrangement, which would have included a further four openings on the angled faces, connecting with the corner-turrets. The spacing between the twelve openings would have been equidistant around the circumference of the circle describing the interior of the lantern.

46   This is seen in section in Figs 31, 32 and 46.

47   Although the situation is confused by the overdrawing of various potential stair arrangements, only two of the turrets are shown with doors providing access from the parapet walks. It may be noted that some other corner-turrets have hollow compartments where they do not contain stairs (*e.g.* in the south transept: turret west of the central gable).

48   Painting in Westminster Abbey Collection; it is unsigned and undated, but on internal evidence must fall within the bracket 1677–1706. Cocke 1995, *op. cit.*, fig. 100.

49   A possible date for the replacement of the ceiling would be 1706, when the sanctuary was refurbished and the enormous Whitehall altarpiece was installed. Cocke 1995, *op. cit.*, 40–3, fig. 22.

50 S. Wren (ed.), *Parentalia*, sect. VII, 295–302 (London, 1750; reprinted Gregg Press, Farnborough, 1965). See also *Wren Soc.* **11**, 15–20.

51 *Wren Soc.* **11**, 18. Grants had been made annually by the House of Commons since 1699.

52 E.B. Chancellor, 'Wren's Restoration of Westminster Abbey: I. The Drawings', *The Connoisseur* **78**, no. 311 (1927), 145–8.

53 *Wren Soc.* **11**, 12. WAM 34511, f. 43. Wren refers to the model in his report of 1713. See also T. Cocke, *900 Years: The Restorations of Westminster Abbey*, 130–1 (Harvey Miller, London, 1995). The date of the model is given there as *c.* 1720.

54 Westminster Abbey, inventory no. 1062. The model has been variously exhibited at the Abbey and elsewhere, and when it was soaked with water during World War II it collapsed. The fragments were subsequently reconstructed by J.G. O'Neilly in *c.* 1980. For a detailed account of its vicissitudes, see T. Platt, *Catalogue of the Lapidarium* (2002), item E22 (WAM, unpublished).

55 *Wren Soc.* **11**, 19.

56 Only two tie-bars are currently missing and these were not linked to the crossing piers, but were associated with the western arcade in the south transept. The physical integration of the east cloister with the western aisle rendered those bars unnecessary anyway.

57 Bodleian Library, Gough Mss. Undated plan (1723, or earlier). Reproduced in *Wren Soc.* **11**, pl. 4.

58 The measurements were taken by Hawksmoor, following the erection of scaffolding in the crossing in April 1724 (p. 47); they are recorded on a piece of paper attached to Wren's drawing of 1715. *Wren Soc.* **11**, 115–16, pl. 4.

59 North-west – 1¾ ins; north-east – 1¼ ins; south-east – ¾ in; south-west – 2¼ ins.

60 *Wren Soc.* **11**, 20. As we see from his other works at the Abbey, Wren's adherence to the Gothic style was anything but strict: he basically invented his own version of Gothic, which had clear classical overtones.

61 *Wren Soc.* **11**, 21.

62 Bodleian Library: Gough Mss. Reproduced in *Wren Soc.* **11**, pl. 4.

63 WAM (P)907. The drawing is dated 14 Sept. 1722.

64 WAM (P)909 with flaps 909A–C. Flap A is dated 4 Aug. 1722 and flap C is dated 8 Jan. 1722/3.

65 WAM (P)909D.
66 Version (iia) was reproduced in *Wren Soc.* **11**, pl. 5.

67 WAM (P)908. The drawing is dated Dec. 1722.

68 WAM (P)911. No explanation can be offered as to why these two, seemingly unrelated, items should have been conjoined and bear the same date.

69 WAM (P)902. *Cf.* Cocke 1995, *op. cit*, fig. 25. The original drawing can be no later than 1720, but the pencilled tower could be a slightly later addition, although the positioning of the image on the paper would argue against that.

70 *Wren Soc.* **11**, 29.

71 North-west view by John James (*Wren Soc.* **11**, 34, 116, pl. 6). A receipt for producing this engraving is dated 13 May 1737 (WAM 46734).

72 W. Maitland, *The History of London*, 686 (London, 1739). The engraving is by W.H. Toms. See also Cocke 1995, *op. cit.*, fig. 24.

73 There is a considerable literature referring to Hawksmoor's contribution to Westminster Abbey. The principal works are: K. Downes, *Hawksmoor* (London, 1959; 2nd edn., 1979); H.M. Colvin, *A Biographical Dictionary of British Architects*, 473–8 (Yale U.P., 3rd edn., 1995); V. Hart, *Nicholas Hawksmoor* (Yale U.P., 2002).

74 Cocke 1995, *op. cit.*, ch. 3.

75 G. Worsley, 'Drawn to a Find', *Country Life* **187** (20 May 1993), 100–1.

76 WAM (P)913. The drawing is neither signed nor dated, but is likely to have been created in 1723 or early in 1724.

77 WAM (P)912. The drawing is neither signed nor dated; several versions of the cupola are indicated on paper flaps.

78 WAM, Hawksmoor drawing no. 5.

79 WAM (P)910, dated May 1724.

80 The legend records: 'The pillars of ye dome are proposed to be fortified and made larger and thicker'.

81 WAM, Hawksmoor drawing no. 4.

82 Drawings in Westminster City Archives: Box 53, nos 6 and 7.

83 Hart 2002, *op. cit.*, figs 55, 81 and 109.

84 Hart 2002, *op. cit.*, 38, fig. 46.

85 WAM 34517; *Wren Soc.* **11**, 29.

86 WAM (P)911.

87 The roof truss shown is characteristically eighteenth century and, as previously remarked, is likely to have been installed by Wren when he was carrying out major roofing work a few years earlier. Self-evidently, several of the drawings considered in this study are structurally 'layered', in that they served both to provide a record of what existed, and at the same time were overlaid with one or more proposals.

88 WAM 34515, f. 25v.

89 WAM, Minutes and Accounts for Repairs, 1722–45. Published in *Wren Soc.* **11**, 30.

90 *Wren Soc.* **11**, 30. The instruction is also recorded on Hawksmoor drawing no. 9.

91 *Wren Soc.* **11**, 30.

92 Westminster Abbey, inventory no. 1043.

93 The significance of the fragments was first identified by Tony Platt, who assembled them for display in the Abbey's former Lapidarium. They have not hitherto been published, and deserve fuller treatment than can be accorded to them here.

94 As reconstructed, this cannot represent the basement stage itself of a wholly octagonal lantern, because the paired windows would have been obstructed by the abutting roofs. On the other hand, since the fragments assembled to form this component are not conjoining, it is possible that they derive from a different structural configuration.

95 The model potentially relates to the western half of the crossing tower, with the stair in the north-west turret, as it is today.

96 WAM, Hawksmoor drawing no. 9.

97 WAM, Hawksmoor drawings nos 10 and 11. Estimates: WAM 34891 and 34892A.

98 WAM, Minutes and Accounts for Repairs, 1722–45. Published in *Wren. Soc.* **11**, 30. For Hawksmoor's estimate, see WAM 34891.

99 WAM 34891 and 34892A. For estimates from the various trades involved, accepted and signed by Hawksmoor, who added the proviso, 'The work is not to exceed this estimate'; see WAM 34688–34693.

100 Most likely, the decision to install a plaster and timber vault over the crossing, rather than the stone one that Hawksmoor preferred, was driven by the need for haste.

101 WAM 34598.

102 WAM 34693 (estimate and instruction to proceed). At this period, Newcastle was noted for the production of the highest quality 'flint' glass in Britain.

103 Engraving by W. & J. Walker, after J. Dixon, dated 30 Jun. 1784, published in *The European Magazine*; copy in the Bodleian Library, Gough Maps, 23, f. 10b; reproduced in T. Friedman, *The Georgian Parish Church: Monuments to Posterity*, fig. 83 (Spire Books, Reading, 2004). There is also a copy of the engraving in WAM.

104 While the view is taken looking east, with the royal box set up in front of the quire screen, the artist seems to have inserted the west window of the nave into the presbytery; it is larger than the windows in the eastern apse, and provided a more satisfactory distant focal point for the viewer. That aside, the architectural detailing is tolerably well recorded.

105 The scheme shown did not just cover the boarded-up arches, but created a continuous frieze around the interior of the tower. Inspiration for this may have been derived from the arcaded gallery-like feature above the external entrance to the north transept: see Hawksmoor drawing no. 4.

106 M. Jourdain, *The Work of William Kent*, 72, fig. 86 (Country Life, London, 1948).

107 The weathering has been altered, and the fourth (topmost) course is a relatively recent addition: it was not present when the 1870s photograph was taken (Fig. 93).

108 WAM, Hawksmoor drawing no. 5. Curiously, this drawing bears two dates and is not readily compatible with the basement stage of the tower that had already been constructed in 1727.

109 WAM 46042. Published in *Wren. Soc.* **11**, 34.

110 WAM, Hawksmoor drawing no. 20.

111 WAM, Minutes and Accounts for Repairs, 1722–45. Published in *Wren. Soc.* **11**, 29.

112 Many artists in the eighteenth and nineteenth centuries chose to omit the tie-bars entirely, but an oil painting (in the Abbey Collection) showing an eastward view of the quire in *c*. 1700 appears to record a full complement of ironwork: it is reproduced in Cocke 1995, *op. cit.*, fig. 100.

113 *Grove Dictionary of Art* (Oxford, 1996).

114 This painting is in the Westminster Abbey Collection.

115 *Ibid.*

116 Christies Auction Catalogue, London, 23 Jun. 1972, lot 2. Photograph in the Conway Library, Courtauld Institute of Art, London (Neg. 625/8/8). The painting was sold by the Rt. Hon. Lord Burnham of Hill Barn, Beaconsfield, and bought by the London art dealer Roy Miles, for 380 guineas (£399). The canvas measured 96.5 x 71.1 cm.

117 For the history of this building, see W. Rodwell in *The Westminster Abbey Chorister* **49** (Winter 2009/10), 21–5.

118 Hawksmoor discussed the work in an undated letter to the dean [1735]: WAM 24878. Published in *Wren. Soc.* **11**, 33–4.

119 Cited in Worsley 1993, *op. cit.*, 101.

120 WAM 34720.

121 Parliament had made the decision in 1697, but the first grant was not paid for another two years. Cocke 1995, *op. cit.*, 48–53.

122 St Margaret's Church is not included in the extracts reproduced here as Figs 79 and 81.

123 The two paintings were acquired separately in the twentieth century: no. 1 found its way to Toynbee Hall, from which it was purchased by Lord Wakefield of Hythe in 1932, and presented to the Dean and Chapter. Painting no. 2 was found hanging in a hotel in the 1930s, by the Keeper of the Muniments of Westminster Abbey, but was then lost from view for many years, turning up again in the 1970s, when it was purchased for the Abbey. See further: L.E. Tanner, *Recollections of a Westminster Antiquary*, 173, pl. 43 (London, 1969).

124 Worsley 1993, *op. cit.*, 100.

125 Copies are held by several institutions, including the British Museum (Prints and Drawings Dept.) and the Guildhall Library, London.

126 Engraving from an unidentified publication. Reproduced in E. Abbott *et al.*, *Westminster Abbey*, 22–3 (Radnor, Pa., USA, 1988). It is there assigned to the late seventeenth century, but is datable to the period 1727–35. It shows the basement for the new lantern tower which was built in 1727, but not the upper part of the north-west tower which was begun in 1735 and completed in 1738.

127 Watercolour in the British Museum: Prints and Drawings 1865-8-10-1323. Reproduced in J. Cherry and N. Stratford, *Westminster Kings and the Medieval Palace of Westminster*, 6. British Museum, Occ. Pap. **115** (1995).

128 *E.g.* R. Ackermann, *The History of St Peter's, Westminster*, **2**, pl. 3 (London, 1812). J.P. Neale and E.W. Brayley, *The History and Antiquities of the Abbey Church of St Peter, Westminster*, **1**, pl. 21; **2**, pls 28 and 41 (London, 1818 and 1823).

129 Woodperry House was built in 1728–31 by John Morse, a wealthy London goldsmith, but he died in 1739 and cannot therefore have commissioned the painting. The chimneypiece was clearly altered to accommodate it, but no plausible connection with subsequent owners or tenants has so far been established.

130 The canvas measures 126 × 70.5 cm; it has been cleaned, rebacked and remounted in recent times.

131 The signature, which is placed in a small plaque on the west face of the tower of St Margaret's Church, occupies three lines: it appears to read MARI[…]F·X / VERV / PINX · A·D·1748. The reading of the second and third lines is not in doubt.

132 For the Woodperry painting, see J. Cornforth, 'Woodperry, Oxfordshire II', *Country Life* **129** (12 Jan. 1961), figs 3 and 12; also M. Airs, 'The Woodperry House Chimney Piece', in M. Airs (ed.), *Baroque and Palladian: The Early Eighteenth-Century Great House*, 47–53 (OUDCE, Oxford, 1996).

133 *E.g.* in the engraving, the north transept, nave and north-west tower all rise from a common base-line, whereas in the painting the true projection of the transept is captured.

134 The fact that the village of Islip lies 3½ miles away from Woodperry – and was the birthplace of Edward the Confessor – hardly provides a convincing explanation for adorning the chimneypiece with a painting of Hawksmoor's design for completing the towers of Westminster Abbey. This has, however, been adumbrated.

135 Illustrations derivative from James's similarly show large lucarnes: *e.g.* E. Walford, *Old and New London*, **3**, 409 (London, 1897; original edn., ed. W. Thornbury, 1872–78).

136 WAM, Chapter Minute Book.

137 It is too much of a coincidence that we have both Kent's estimate for painting figures, and a view showing an arcaded gallery that would have housed them: the evidence is complementary, and I am not therefore inclined to reject out-of-hand either element as having never existed in reality.

138 The interior of the lantern is also just glimpsed in Malton's view of the nave. Engravings in Westminster Abbey. WA Lib., Langley Coll. II.1.(22). Cocke 1995, *op. cit.*, figs 36 and 37.

139 J. Perkins, *Westminster Abbey: Its Worship and Ornaments*, **1**, 149. Alcuin Club Coll. (London, 1938).

140 J. Carter, letter in *Gentleman's Magazine* **73**(ii) (1803), 636–8.

141 Carter criticized this unhistorical approach in *Gentleman's Magazine* **75**(i) (1805), 324.

142 Neale and Brayley, **2** (1823), *op. cit.*, pls 33 and 45.

143 Ackermann, **2** (1812), *op. cit.*, pls 7 and 9. Neale and Brayley, **2** (1823), pl. 42. Cocke 1995, *op. cit.*, fig. 38. Note: Ackermann's pl. 9 (1811)shows no door in the filling of the northern arch, which would appear to be a consequence of his copying the view from Malton's painting of 1793; that being pre-fire, the aperture was merely boarded over.

144 The boarding was fixed to the backs of the arches, so that they appeared as recesses when viewed from the crossing. Remains of the iron cleats that held the boarding are visible inside the roofs spaces.

145 Access for repair and maintenance was difficult, since there was not even a parapet around the top of the tower.

146 On the right-hand side of the bricked-up arch in the west face of the tower.

147 G.G. Scott, *Gleanings from Westminster Abbey*, 37 (2nd edn., London, 1863).

148 Scott built the present crossing tower and spire at Chichester Cathedral, following the collapse of the medieval one in 1861, he carried out major restorations on towers and spires at Salisbury, Lichfield and other cathedrals in the 1860s and 1870s, and he designed new churches such as the twin-towered and spired Episcopalian Cathedral at Edinburgh (1876).

149 For details of this and other works carried out by Scott and later Surveyors, see C. Reynolds (ed.), *Reports and Letters of the Surveyors of the Fabric, Westminster Abbey, 1827–1906* (forthcoming).

150 G.G. Scott, *Personal and Professional Recollections by the Late Sir Gilbert Scott, R.A., Edited by his son, G. Gilbert Scott, F.S.A.*, 153. (London, 1879; new edn., Stamford, 1995).

151 The instruction to carry out this work was given to Samuel Cundy, stonemason, on 26 Feb. 1859: Scott's report to the Dean and Chapter. WAM, RCO 5.

152 The windows were installed by Cundy, whose contract is dated 21 Mar. 1859. WAM, RCO 5.

153 WAM, RCO 5.

154 S. Brindle, 'Sir George Gilbert Scott and the Restoration of the Chapter House, 1849–72', in Rodwell and Mortimer 2010, *op. cit.*, 139–57.

155 For an undated drawing (late nineteenth century?) of the proposed layout of the roof leads, see WAM, SD/1/596.

156 G.G. Scott 1879, *op. cit.*, 287. See also A.D.C. Hyland, 'Imperial Valhalla', *Journ. Soc. Architectural Historians* **21** (1962), 129–39.

157 WAM, RCO 6; dated 11 Feb. 1899.

158 For the context of these schemes, see G.A. Bremner, '"Imperial Monumental Halls and Tower": Westminster Abbey and the Commemoration of Empire, 1854–1904', *Architectural History* **47** (2004), 251–82.

159 A series of views was prepared; two of the watercolours are in the RIBA Drawings Collection at the Victoria and Albert Museum.

160 The architects proposed only a single, large belfry opening in each face of the crossing tower; this is unusual, there being more commonly two openings per face. In that respect they took their cue from the Abbey's western towers, where the principal faces are smaller on account of the heavy buttressing.

161 W. Rodwell, 'The Chapter House Glazing', in Rodwell and Mortimer 2010, *op. cit.*, 250, fig. 239.

162 This occurred in the presence of A.L.N. Russell, architect for Westminster School: *The Guardian*, 12 May 1941. The report is probably exaggerated, since very little masonry was dislodged by the fire.

163 WAM, Peers's files include design drawings of the new roof structure, dated July 1941.

164 Inf. from Alan Rome, former Assistant Surveyor under Dykes Bower. I have been unable to trace a copy of this photograph.

165 WAM, SD/1/635–639.

166 The unfortunate effect is well demonstrated in a photograph taken in May 1945 at a service celebrating Britain's victory in the Second World War (press cutting kindly supplied by Alan Rome).

167 This pavement, comprising diagonally-laid squares of black and white marble, was first laid in 1677, repaired in 1746, taken up and relaid in 1775–76 when the quire was reordered, patched after the fire of 1803, taken up and relaid again in 1847, and finally repaired in 1957.

168 WAM, the Dykes Bower files contain considerable correspondence relating to post-war repairs. For

dimensioned survey drawings (May 1956) of the interior of the lantern, see WAM, SD/1/678–679.

169   WAM, Dykes Bower files. The cost of the glazing was £1,514 10*s* 0*d*, plus £368 for scaffolding.

170   The structural engineer who designed the ceiling support was H.J. Paton. His drawings (dated 30 May 1956) and correspondence are in WAM.

171   WAM, Dykes Bower files. Letter from Mathew to the Librarian, 28 Sept. 1984.

172   WAM, SD/1/600–602, 698–806.

173   It is also found earlier in the wallpainting in St Faith's chapel.

174   Dr E. Clive Rouse advised on the painting (inf. from Dr Pamela Tudor-Craig).

175   By Peter Foster, Surveyor of the Fabric, 1973–88. WAM, SD/1/879–881.

176   Surveys carried out by The Downland Partnership Ltd, using a combination of techniques: GIS surveying, photogrammetry and laser-scanning.

177   The amounts by which the piers are out of plumb are as follows: south-west, 2.2 cm; north-west, 8.4 cm; north-east, 2.7 cm; south-east, 0.5 cm. The bowing on the full height of the shafts is, respectively, 8.6 cm, 8.3 cm, 8.2 cm and 7.1 cm.

178   The crossing has been analyzed by Clive Richardson, Structural Engineer to Westminster Abbey, who has very kindly supplied the data incorporated in this chapter.

179   A pit was dug against the transept foundation in 1869, when some information about the raft and local ground conditions was noted, albeit very sketchily: H. Poole, 'Some Account of the Discovery of the Roman Coffin in the North Green of Westminster Abbey', *Archaeol. Journ.* **27** (1870), 119–46; see esp. 124 and plan opp. 118.

180   WAM, SD/1/634.

181   Mr Richardson points out that, in making his calculations, certain reasonable assumptions had to be made where absolute knowledge is lacking.

182   Carried out by Mrs Erica Utsi, of Utsi Electronics Ltd.

183   For a plan showing the topographical relationship between the medieval Palace and the Abbey, see Thomas *et al.* 2006, *op. cit.*, fig. 45.

184   This appendix is largely based on the author's article, 'Staged Timber Spires in Carolingian North-east France and Late Anglo-Saxon England', *Journ. British Archaeol. Assoc.* **148** (1995), 29–54, where full references will be found.

Index

Bold type indicates a figure reference